*A TA's Guide to Teaching
Writing in All Disciplines*

A TA's Guide to Teaching Writing in All Disciplines

Beth Finch Hedengren
Brigham Young University

BEDFORD/ST. MARTIN'S   BOSTON ♦ NEW YORK

For Bedford/St. Martin's

Developmental Editor: Gregory S. Johnson
Senior Production Editor: Shuli Traub
Production Supervisor: Dennis J. Conroy
Copy Editor: Sally Scott
Cover Design: Donna Lee Dennison
Composition: Pageworks
Printing and Binding: Haddon Craftsmen, Inc., an R. R. Donnelley & Sons
    Company

President: Joan E. Feinberg
Editorial Director: Denise B. Wydra
Editor in Chief: Nancy Perry
Director of Marketing: Karen Melton Soeltz
Director of Editing, Design, and Production: Marcia Cohen
Managing Editor: Erica T. Appel

Library of Congress Control Number: 2003111067

Manufactured in the United States of America

9 8
f e

For information, write: Bedford/St. Martin's, 75 Arlington Street, Boston, MA
02116   (617-399-4000)

ISBN-10: 0-312-40714-9
ISBN-13: 978-0-312-40714-8

Acknowledgments

Susan McLeod and Elaine Maimon. Excerpt from "Clearing the Air: WAC
Myths and Realities." From *College English* 62.5, May 2000. Copyright © 2000 by
the National Council of Teachers of English. Reprinted with permission.

Laren M. Tolbert and Kyril M. Solntsev. Excerpt from "Excited-State Proton
Transfer: From Constrained Systems to 'Super' Photoacids to Superfast Proton
Transfer." Reprinted in part with permission from *Accounts of Chemical Re-
search* 35.1, 2002. Copyright © 2002 American Chemical Society.

The Far Side ® by Gary Larson © 1994 FarWorks, Inc. All rights reserved. Used
with permission.

PEANUTS reprinted by permission of United Features Syndicate, Inc.

Preface for Faculty

As one of the lucky professors with teaching assistants (TAs) for your course, you probably realize the great value of having these capable, advanced students work with you. TAs are a bridge between you and your students, accessible mentors who can explain concepts to undergraduates. They also, of course, assist you with tasks ranging from the simple to the complex. Most relevant to this book, TAs often help students with the writing required for the class—providing tutorials, responding to drafts, answering questions to clarify assignments, and even evaluating students' writing.

However, TAs are chosen because of their expertise in a particular discipline—not because they have been trained to teach or evaluate writing—and so you might be concerned about your TAs knowing enough about writing to help students or to evaluate students' writing consistently and fairly. Professors I polled worried that "TAs should have superior writing skill and many times they don't" and that "TAs are not trained in writing, teaching, or evaluating." *A TA's Guide to Teaching Writing in All Disciplines,* which can serve as a text for a TA training course or a reference for TAs to use on their own, is an effort to alleviate such concerns.

This short book and its companion Web site, <bedfordstmartins.com/ta_guide>, provide TAs with the information, techniques, examples, and advice they need to teach and evaluate writing effectively—no matter the discipline. Part I of this book, "What You Teach When You Teach Writing," discusses Writing to Learn, writing across the curriculum, and the various steps of the writing process. Included in Part I are specific strategies TAs can use to help students with all aspects of writing, from understanding the assignment and generating ideas to editing for correctness and sharing writing with an audience. Part II, "Ways to Teach Writing," focuses on how to conduct one-on-one conferences and in-class workshops, as well as how to prepare students for essay exams, research papers, and collaborative writing projects. Also included in Part II are strategies for commenting on and evaluating papers, dealing with plagiarism, and maintaining professionalism. The book closes with advice on using time well, and throughout there are helpful teaching tips and tactics for incorporating technology into the subject-based classroom. The Web site features an online glossary of writing-related terms, as well as downloadable versions of the book's sample assignments, grading rubrics, and planning sheets.

Having a TA is a great opportunity, but it is also a responsibility that *A TA's Guide* will help you manage. I hope that you will read this book along with your TAs and refer to each chapter's "Working with Your Professor" section, which features suggestions for discussing that chapter's concepts. These discussion prompts will facilitate communication between you and your TAs and enable you to check on their progress. In addition to this book, the "TA Training Course" at <bedfordstmartins.com/ta_guide> provides information on how to use *A TA's*

Guide in a TA training course, including suggested schedules, group training activities, and tips for maintaining effective professor-TA relationships. Though teaching assistants are employees, they are also students, so take the time to help your teaching assistants learn the skills they need.

Acknowledgments

I could not have completed this book without the support of many colleagues and students. Kristine Hansen, Associate Dean of Undergraduate Education, University Writing, has taught me much about writing across the curriculum as we worked together in the program at Brigham Young University, as well as mentoring and encouraging my work with TAs. I also learned much about teaching TAs from my colleagues Susan Miller and Ana Preto-Bay, who collaborated with me on many TA workshops. In addition, Ana Preto-Bay provided invaluable feedback on the manuscript of this book.

Many faculty at BYU have contributed to my understanding of writing in the various disciplines. I am especially thankful to Cory Barker, Donna Lee Bowen, Eric Christiansen, Brian Harker, Suzanne Hendrix, Jeff Keith, Darl Larson, Jeannette Lawler, Alison Lemon, David Nelson, Nora Nyland, Jenny Pulsipher, Lee Robinson, Megan Sanborn Jones, Kylie Turley, and Steven Wood for allowing me to include their excellent discipline-specific assignments and examples in this book. Thanks to our secretary Laura Paulson Howe for her encouragement and assistance throughout this project.

I must give special thanks to my Fall 2002 class of Writing Fellow trainees, a cross-disciplinary group of bright undergraduates, many of whom also worked as TAs. The class kindly read my manuscript and offered invaluable help in making revision decisions. I must especially thank Amanda Alleman, Scott Fitzgerald, Paul Morrison, Sarah Olson, and Marin Turley, students who contributed discipline-specific examples to use in this book.

The following professionals and TAs read the manuscript thoroughly and provided careful and insightful advice: Chandima Abeywickrama, Queens College (TA in chemistry); Alexis Blackmer, University of California–Davis (TA in neurobiology); Glenn Blalock, Texas A & M University–Corpus Christi; Will Davis, University of California–Davis; Cinthia Gannett, University of New Hampshire; Joan Graham, University of Washington; Maren Harding, Texas A & M University–Corpus Christi (TA in biology); Mary Hocks, Georgia State University; Christa Jiamachello, University of Toledo (TA in philosophy); David Kellogg, Duke University; Richard Lange, University of Toledo (TA in music); Jeffrey Mahan, Texas A & M University–Corpus Christi (TA in history); Sarah Miller, University of Toledo (TA in history); Joan Mullin, University of Toledo; Terry Myers Zawacki, George Mason University; and Art Young, Clemson University. I am very grateful for their comments, which greatly influenced my revisions.

Many thanks are due to Nancy Perry and Greg Johnson of Bedford/St. Martin's for their invaluable support and professional guidance throughout the production of this book and to Kristy Bredin for her work on the Web site. Greg has been a particularly insightful and skilled collaborator throughout the editing process.

Finally I must thank my husband, Paul Hedengren, and my children—Anna Dunn, Emily Lyman, David Hedengren, Mark Hedengren, and Mary Hedengren —all of whom read portions of the manuscript and encouraged me in every way. I could not have completed this project without their support.

Beth Finch Hedengren
Brigham Young University

Preface for TAs

If you are a teaching assistant who has been asked to teach or evaluate writing in a subject-based course, you may be thinking, "Hey! I'm not an English major," but this is the very reason why you are qualified to teach writing in your particular discipline. As someone who has experience learning and writing in your field, you are in an ideal position to help the students you will be teaching to move to the next level of writing development. And *A TA's Guide to Teaching Writing in All Disciplines* and its companion Web site, <bedfordstmartins.com/ta_guide>, will provide you with the information, techniques, examples, and advice you need to feel confident about teaching and evaluating writing effectively.

Part I, "What You Teach When You Teach Writing," explains why writing matters in a subject-based course and how to use the steps of the writing process to teach students how to write, from understanding the assignment and generating ideas to editing for correctness and sharing writing with an audience. Part II, "Ways to Teach Writing," focuses on how to conduct one-on-one conferences and in-class workshops, as well as how to prepare students for essay exams, research papers, and collaborative writing projects. Also included in Part II are strategies for commenting on and evaluating papers, dealing with plagiarism, and maintaining professionalism. The Web site features an online glossary of writing-related terms, as well as downloadable versions of the book's sample assignments, grading rubrics, and planning sheets.

In addition, the Teaching Tip, Technology Tactics, and Chapter Checklist boxes throughout this book provide quick, at-a-glance information and summaries. The "Applications to Your Own Situation" and "Working with Your Professor" sections at the end of each chapter will help you apply each chapter's concepts and facilitate communication between you and your professor.

Being a TA can be a wonderful learning experience, but it is also a responsibility. *A TA's Guide to Teaching Writing in All Disciplines* will help you manage this responsibility. For more information on the features of and how to use *A TA's Guide* and its companion Web site, see Chapter 1, "Getting Started—How to Use This Book."

Beth Finch Hedengren
Brigham Young University

Contents

Part I: What You Teach When You Teach Writing

CHAPTER 11

Fair and Consistent Evaluation   102

CHAPTER 12

Essay Exams, Research Papers, and Collaborative Writing Projects   114

CHAPTER 13

Plagiarism and Other Grading-Related Concerns   127

What You Teach When You Teach Writing

Getting Started—How to Use This Book

"True ease in writing comes from art not chance,
As those move easiest who have learned to dance."

—Alexander Pope, "Essay on Criticism"

In this chapter you will learn

- how this book will help you teach and evaluate writing in your discipline.
- about the features of this book and how to use them.
- what online resources are available to you at <bedfordstmartins.com/ta_guide> and how to use them.

Congratulations on landing that prestigious job of teaching assistant! You must be pretty capable in your subject, for professors choose TAs only from the most talented, knowledgeable students they know. You may be feeling a bit apprehensive about teaching others the material you aced on an exam in some previous semester, but you know you can probably handle it.

You may be feeling a little nervous about the writing assignments you will be expected to teach and evaluate, however. Even if you write well yourself, you may not understand why your writing is good or even be conscious of the process you follow when you write. And if you are in a field like chemistry or physics, where you haven't written much in your major classes, you may be wondering if you even know where to begin to teach novice chemists or physicists how to write. You may feel like the TA who told me, "I'm worried I'm inadequate in my abilities" or the one who admitted, "I'm not the greatest writer myself." Another TA worried that "students wouldn't trust me as a writing helper."

If you are a TA for whom English is not your native language, you may feel especially apprehensive. Although you are clearly bright and capable, you may not have a native speaker's instinctive grasp of grammar and mechanics. Even the expectations for format and structure differ from culture to culture, and you may feel insecure about requirements for English writing in your field.

The purpose of this book is to help all TAs feel more confident about helping students with writing. You may be thinking, "Hey! I'm not an English major," but this is the very reason why you are most qualified to teach writing in your particular discipline. As a student who has had more experience learning and writing in this subject than the students in your class, you are in an ideal position to help them move along to the next level of their writing development.

About This Book

You don't have to be a great writer to be a good writing teacher, but you do need to know the principles behind good writing and certain techniques for teaching them. Writing is like math, physics, chemistry, or history: You need to learn the theory and practice the technique. This book will help you learn the nuts and bolts of writing theory and evaluation. It will also help you apply that theory to your particular discipline and your particular teaching situation.

WRITING THEORY

All writing exists for the purpose of communicating, and good writers know that in order to communicate well they must consider their purpose, their audience, and the overall context of their particular communication—what theorists call the *rhetorical situation.* This rhetorical understanding will help students write within a certain disciplinary context and will prepare you to help novice writers approach writing tasks. If you understand what makes writing good on the global level (focus, structure, support) and the local level (paragraphing, mechanics, usage), you will also be better able to guide your students.

Part I of this book, "What You Teach When You Teach Writing," provides easily accessible, basic information on—and application of—writing theory. This section will help you lead students through the process of understanding the requirements of a writing assignment and finding an idea to write about (Chapter 3, "Prewriting") to polishing their writing (Chapter 6, "Editing") to handing in their final papers (Chapter 7, "Publishing"). This section also includes background information on the Writing Across the Curriculum (WAC) movement and why writing instruction occurs in subject-based courses (Chapter 2, "Why [and How] We Teach Writing"). The many useful techniques, exercises, and examples in this section will help you understand the writing process, one's rhetorical situation, and the requirements of writing done in a particular genre for a particular discipline.

TEACHING TECHNIQUES

As a TA you will be responsible for teaching students how to write in a variety of situations. You may teach certain concepts to groups of students, either as part of class time or in out-of-class help sessions. You will undoubtedly help students with their writing in one-on-one conferences during your office hours. It is quite likely that your professor will have you write comments on student papers or perhaps even evaluate those papers.

Part II of this book, "Ways to Teach Writing," specifically addresses teaching situations you will likely face—such as helping students in one-on-one conferences and in-class workshops (Chapters 8 and 9), commenting on and evaluating students' papers fairly and consistently (Chapters 10 and 11), and addressing plagiarism and other grading-related concerns (Chapter 13)—and provides practical advice for dealing with them. In addition, this section includes a chapter that addresses assigning and evaluating specialized types of writing (Chapter 12), as well as chapters on maintaining professionalism (Chapter 14) and doing the job of a TA effectively (Chapter 15).

Book Features

As you read this book, you will notice that each chapter contains boxes and sets of questions or activities. These features will help you use *A TA's Guide to Teaching Writing in All Disciplines* as a resource and reference. They also contain ideas to help you personalize and apply each chapter's concepts and techniques to your own situation.

- **Chapter openers.** Each chapter opens with a bulleted list of what you will learn, providing you with a quick preview of each chapter's contents.

- **Technology Tactics boxes.** Appearing in every chapter, these helpful boxes feature suggestions for using technology, computers, and the Internet to augment your instruction and to get students involved with their own learning and writing.

- **Teaching Tip boxes.** These informative boxes contain a variety of ideas, tips, and suggestions for applying each chapter's concepts to your own teaching.

- **Examples.** Throughout this book you will find examples that illustrate concepts put into practice, such as grading rubrics, assignment sheets, and planning worksheets.

- **Chapter Checklist boxes.** These quick references at the end of each chapter summarize the chapter's main points in an easy-to-follow checklist format. Refer to them as brief refreshers of each chapter's key concepts.

- **"Applications to Your Own Situation."** These end-of-chapter activities help you put concepts into practice. Refer to these sections for ideas on how to develop your own ways to teach certain skills and address your particular students' concerns.

- **"Working with Your Professor."** Each chapter closes with a list of suggestions for creating a dialogue between you and your professor. Refer to these sections for ideas on how to approach your professor to ask questions or talk about your class and students.

- **Bibliography.** The bibliography at the end of this book lists professional resources from Bedford/St. Martin's, writing handbooks, discipline-specific writing guides, discipline-specific style and documentation guides, general style and editing guides, and teaching resources and references.

Web Site Features

In addition to the print version of this book, the following resources are available to you online at <bedfordstmartins.com/ta_guide>.

- **Glossary.** This is an online, hyperlinked glossary of grammar- and writing-related terms. Refer to it as needed as you read this book or encounter unfamiliar terms in your day-to-day instruction.

- **Grading rubrics.** Grading rubrics and assignment sheets featured in this book are available for download. Use them as models for drafting your own rubrics or, to spark discussion about your particular assignments and grading guidelines, share them with your professor.

- **TA training course.** Written for faculty members, this Web-only feature includes information on how to use *A TA's Guide to Teaching Writing in All Disciplines* in a TA training course. Refer your professor to this online resource.

- **Overview of the writing process.** This overview provides a brief explanation of each step of the writing process, from prewriting to publishing.

- **Annotated links.** This collection of annotated links provides access to TA support and teaching resources on the Web.

- **Downloadable forms and worksheets.** Blank versions of the planning forms and worksheets contained in this book are available for download. Use these materials to help plan a group workshop, draft writing assignment instructions, or develop other writing activities.

- **The Bedford/St. Martin's Workshop on Plagiarism.** This site features downloadable handouts on plagiarism for students and instructors, information on how to use writing portfolios and online discussion forums to avoid plagiarism, links to full-text articles about plagiarism and the Internet, and links to other Bedford/St. Martin's workshops and online professional resources.

- **Research and Documentation Online.** This site features guidelines and models for documenting print and online sources in MLA, APA, *Chicago,* and CBE styles; sample documented student papers; and annotated links to discipline-specific research sites.

Conclusion

As you prepare to do this work, remember that you are a teaching *assistant,* which means you are employed to assist the professor. In order to do that well, you must coordinate with him or her and understand course expectations. You need to understand the purpose behind every writing assignment. And this book will help you do just that.

But perhaps more important than any knowledge or resource is your attitude as a teacher. As Peter Elbow, one of the foremost authorities in teaching writing, said, "Good writing teachers [and good TAs] like students' writing (and like students)."[1] The most important part of being a good writing teacher is an attitude of respect for the students you teach, an appreciation for their ideas and their writing.

Enjoy this opportunity. As you help students with writing, you will learn more about writing yourself. As you respond to students' written ideas about your subject, you will come to a much fuller understanding of the subject matter yourself. And as you help students learn to express themselves better, you will have the satisfaction of seeing them grow in comprehension and confidence. You'll experience the deep pleasure of teaching *well*.

Chapter Checklist

☐ Use this book as a resource for information and skills that will help you teach writing. Read the book through early in the semester. Go back to appropriate chapters to review techniques and concepts as needed.

☐ Use this book's features—the boxes and end-of-chapter material—to personalize and apply the techniques and concepts in this book. As needed, use the online resources provided on this book's companion Web site, <bedfordsmartins.com/ta_guide>.

☐ Regularly discuss with your professor your class, students, and concepts from this book.

☐ Be patient with students and respect them.

Applications to Your Own Situation

1. Write for five minutes about how you feel about helping students with writing. What are your fears? What do you think you have to offer a student as a writing teacher?

2. Look through the Bibliography at the end of this book. Which handbooks and writing guides do you think would be useful? Check your own bookshelf. What resources do you already own? What other resources would be helpful for the particular class you are TAing? Make a plan for collecting the resources you need to help your students with writing in your class.

3. Think of TAs you worked with when you were a student. What bad experiences did you have? What good experiences? Divide a sheet of paper into two columns. List the qualities of a bad TA on one side, the qualities of a good TA on the other. Circle the good qualities you want to work on.

Working with Your Professor

1. Find out exactly what your duties will be as a TA for the class. Ask your professor what he or she expects you to do to help students with

writing. Will you teach students in groups and/or in individual conferences? Will you respond to students' writing? Evaluate students' writing?

2.   Ask your professor what resources would help you teach writing in your discipline. Can he or she recommend a particular style or documentation guide or provide some good models of student writing in your discipline? Ask your professor how he or she teaches writing in your discipline.

CHAPTER 2

Why (and How) We Teach Writing

"Writing is thinking on paper."

—William Zinsser, *On Writing Well*

In this chapter you will learn

- how the Writing-Across-the-Curriculum movement developed.
- how Writing-to-Learn assignments help students understand and remember material.
- how Writing in the Disciplines improves students' comprehension and fosters understanding of discipline-specific writing genres and conventions.
- how to use the writing process to teach writing.

"Yes," you may be thinking, "I see that this book will help me to teach and evaluate writing as a TA. But why does writing matter in a subject such as chemistry, political science, or physics anyway? After all, doesn't writing belong in an English course? And how does a non-English teacher teach writing?" An explanation of the theory underlying Writing Across the Curriculum (WAC) and the writing process will help you understand why writing is essential in subject-area courses and how *you* can teach writing.

Writing Across the Curriculum (WAC)

Writing Across the Curriculum (WAC) refers to the writing students do in all their classes. The WAC movement recognizes that students cannot learn all they need to know about writing in one or two semesters of required composition classes. As with all skills, writing ability improves with practice. Students need to practice writing throughout their university careers in order to improve as writers. Besides, writing in disciplinary classes has a number of benefits for both professors and students. At a meeting recently I asked faculty from all disciplines why they wanted to include writing assignments in their courses. They immediately responded with comments such as the following:

- "When I read what my students have written, I can see what they have really learned."

- "I just came from working in industry as an accountant. All I did was write reports. I need to teach my students to write so they will be prepared for the work they will do."

These comments reflect the two main reasons for including Writing Across the Curriculum: Writing to Learn and Writing in the Disciplines.

WRITING TO LEARN

Perhaps the most important reason to include writing in the subject-based classroom is that writing actually helps students learn and remember material. For example, how well do you remember dates or formulas you learned for an objective test you took three years ago? In contrast, how well do you remember the information you researched for a paper you wrote three years ago? Most people remember the content of their own writing much better than the facts they studied to pass an exam.

In her landmark 1977 study, "Writing as a Mode of Learning," composition expert Janet Emig compared learning theory research with writing practices and found that writing facilitates effective learning because it uses many senses (sight, touch, hearing), is both analytic and creative, provides a product that is available for both immediate and long-term feedback, uses syntax and paragraphing that force synthesis and analysis, and requires an active engagement with the material.[1] Toby Fulwiler, another composition scholar, provides an even simpler summary of why writing enhances learning: It is physical, visible, and personal.[2]

This learning enhancement is certainly accomplished through major, formal writing assignments such as research papers, but much good can also be derived from informal and even extremely brief writings. The writing may take place during class or outside of class as a homework assignment. Any brief writing assignment will center students' attention on the subject at hand. Having students write even for one minute—summarizing the content of the day's lecture or composing a question about the material—serves the purpose of physically, visibly, and personally enhancing students' learning. Writing assignments are most likely to increase learning when they have been designed with that purpose in mind.

Teaching Tip: In-Class Writing-to-Learn Activities

Writing-to-Learn assignments might take only a few minutes out of a class period. Asking students to write brief responses to simple prompts can provide information about student learning, encourage student participation, and help students to synthesize course information. Below are some ideas for short writing prompts.

At the beginning of class, students might write for a few minutes on one of the following prompts. Have students share their responses with the class to start the day's discussion.

- What questions do you have about last night's reading?
- What's the relationship between yesterday's topic and today's?
- What were the most important points in last night's reading?

During the middle of the class, students might take a few minutes to respond to one of the following prompts. Ask a couple of students to share their responses to check understanding and refocus the class on the course material.

- Summarize the concept we've been discussing in class today.
- What questions do you still have about this material?

At the end of class, ask students to write on one of the following questions. Have them pass in their responses as they leave the classroom. As a TA you can scan through the responses and let your professor know whatever problems the students are having with comprehension. Then your professor can adapt the next lesson to meet the particular needs of the students.

- What's the most significant thing you've learned in class today?
- What aspect of this concept confuses you?
- Explain what we learned today in your own words.

Writing-to-Learn assignments can also be specifically tailored to a particular course. For example, the following list features Writing-to-Learn assignments used by faculty members in a number of disciplines at Brigham Young University.[i]

- **Audiology and Speech Language Pathology.** For each game or art project studied, students write down one therapy idea and describe how they would use it with current clients.
- **Geology.** For a ten-minute in-class essay, students are given some statements for and against population control. They write about this question: "Do present-day environmental concerns justify government-sponsored measures to halt population growth?" After writing, students exchange essays and write a brief response to their classmates' essays. Then they exchange essays again and write another response, so every student receives two responses.
- **History.** For homework, students write a one-paragraph-length question to be turned in at the beginning of each class period. Questions make up 20 percent of the course grade and will be evaluated according to quality of thought and appropriateness for stimulating class discussion.

---

[i]Thanks to Lee Robinson, Jeff Keith, Jenny Pulsipher, Brian Harker, and Suzanne Hendrix.

- **Music.** After listening to Beethoven's Appassionata Sonata, Movement 1, students write for five minutes on this prompt: "Pretend you are Antonio Salieri. How would you react to this piece? Why?"
- **Statistics.** Students write, in their own words, a one- to two-sentence explanation of the central limit theorem.

Journals or learning logs—in which students write an entry every class period or every week—can be used as ongoing Writing-to-Learn assignments. The prompt can remain constant (a summary for every reading assignment) or variable (a different question provided for students to respond to in each class period). In either case, writing in a journal regularly will assure that students not only complete class assignments, but also *think* about them. They will come to class more prepared to listen to the lecture and contribute to discussion. However, it is very important that students see the journal assignments as clearly reinforcing what they are learning in class and not just as busy work. Students' writings should be read, responded to, and evaluated in some way.[ii] Example 2.1 is a reading journal assignment, and Example 2.2 is the journal assignment's corresponding template for students' written responses.

A Writing-to-Learn assignment could also be a short, relatively easy-to-grade essay, or micro-theme, that would require students' thoughtful analysis and synthesis of the material. See Example 2.3 for a particularly creative micro-theme assignment from an introductory chemistry class.

EXAMPLE 2.1.   Reading Journal Assignment[iii]

NDFS 440—READING JOURNAL	
Purpose	The reading journal should do two things. First, it will encourage you stay on top of the reading assignments. Second, by thinking and writing about the reading material, you should have a much better grasp of the ideas, concepts, and principles of management in dietetics than you otherwise would.
Audience	You are really writing to and for yourself, but I will look at your entries, and your question section might be written to me or to yourself. Occasionally you will share and compare entries with your classmates.
Format	A template is provided for you in the syllabus and you can download the template from the Web. Diagrams may be neatly done by hand, but please type other parts of your entry. Examples of diagrams are shown below.

[ii] *The Journal Book* by Toby Fulwiler contains useful information on creating, assigning, and evaluating functional journal assignments; see the Bibliography.

[iii] Thanks to Nora Nyland, Department of Nutrition, Dietetics, and Food Science, Brigham Young University (BYU).

Fish diagram	Organization chart
Cluster	Map

Volume	You will need at least one page per week. Sometimes the reading assignments for the week are closely related and can be put on one form. Some weeks, however, the reading topics are different enough to warrant two forms.
Due dates	Journal entries are due, generally at the beginning of the class period, when "RJ" is shown on the schedule.
Evaluation	Journal entries will be five (5) points each. An entry displaying obvious lack of thought (which includes looking too much like a classmate's entry) will result in the loss of three (3) points. Journal entries will not be accepted after the class period ends—they must be turned in when called for in class.

EXAMPLE 2.2.   Reading Journal Response Template[iv]

NDFS 440—READING JOURNAL RESPONSE TEMPLATE	
Name:_____ Date:_____ Section:_____ Responding to:_____	
Summary, outline, or diagram of key concepts: Use this area to: ■ Summarize—use prose to condense the reading into short but salient points. ■ Outline key points using standard outline format.	**So . . .** Think about the reading assignment and in this space answer questions like: *(continued)*

[iv]Thanks to Nora Nyland, Department of Nutrition, Dietetics, and Food Science, BYU.

EXAMPLE 2.2. *(continued)*

■ Diagram the important points using a fish diagram, cluster, map, or organization chart.	■ How does this relate to previous reading or class discussion? ■ Have I observed these principles in action (or being violated)? ■ Why is this information important to know? Or make other associations or observations related to the reading.

I'm not sure about:

List concepts that are not clear to you, connections you aren't sure of, or other questions raised by the reading.

Example 2.3. Micro-theme Assignment[v]

CHEM 105—MICRO-THEME ASSIGNMENT #5	
Purpose	To understand the physical states or phases of matter and intermolecular forces (especially hydrogen bonding).
Point of view	A water molecule.
Audience	Fellow water molecules.
Scenario	You are a single water molecule among many in a hot water heater. All of a sudden, you are released from the water heater tank and violently expelled through the

---

[v]Thanks to Steven Wood, Department of Chemistry and Biochemistry, BYU.

	nozzle of a showerhead. Before you recover, however, you are alone for a period of time, until you meet a group of your water molecule friends on the surface of a bathroom mirror.
Writing assignment	One the surface of the mirror, you and your friends all share similar stories. Since you are the most scientifically inclined of the group, you are assigned to write a short report, based on sound fundamental molecular reasoning, explaining what happened to you all. Your report to the group should include a discussion of the forces that kept you all together and then reunited you. You should also explain why you each found yourselves alone for a period of time and how you ended up together again on the surface of the mirror. A couple of good paragraphs should suffice.
Focusing questions	You will need to formulate these as part of the prewriting analysis. Be sure to point out the inner-relationship between the physical states of matter and intermolecular forces, giving special attention to hydrogen bonding.

Designing Writing-to-Learn Assignments

Whether you use in-class writings, a daily journal, or micro-themes, Writing-to-Learn assignments are good ways to involve students in their own learning and for you and your professor to quickly gauge how well the students understand the material. The following are some guidelines to consider as you and your professor design your own Writing-to-Learn assignments.

- **Integrate the writing into the course work.** Use the students' writing in class so that it carries importance. Have the students discuss the writing in small groups or use the writing as test preparation. Read aloud some of the writing to the class, or have the students use this informal writing to prepare for a formal writing assignment. Read through the students' responses to get an idea of their understanding of the material, so your professor can adjust the lectures accordingly. Be sure that the students understand how writing fits into the rest of the course work. You and your professor should know what you hope to accomplish through the writing assignment. Share these goals with the students.

- **Decide on clear guidelines for each assignment.** You need a clear writing prompt to guide the students' writing. Let the students know how long they should take (one minute? five? twenty?). Tell them whether or not you will be checking for surface, mechanical errors. Let the students know the form of the writing (a question? journal entry? list?) and the audience (classmates? you? the professor?). Explain whether you will collect the writing and if you will give credit for it.

- **Be sure that the students get some kind of feedback on their writing.** Depending on the assignment, the feedback could be a brief comment from you on the page or notes from a classmate in a small group discussion. If you don't have time to review every piece of writing, you could read and respond to these brief assignments randomly—looking at only five out of ten papers. The students need not know which entries will be read. For very brief "one-minute" papers, you could ask for volunteers to read aloud what they have written. Students want their writing to be read. Otherwise they see the writing as simply "busy work."

Exploratory kinds of writing assignments force your students to think about the information, make applications, synthesize, and analyze. Short in-class writing assignments, journal assignments, or electronic postings are just a few ways to use writing as a learning tool in just about any class. Writing to enhance learning is one very important reason to include writing in a subject-based class.

Technology Tactics

Using email messages and online discussion groups can be an efficient means of encouraging Writing to Learn. The technology encourages all students to participate, even shy ones who may not raise their hands in a classroom. Try one of the following assignments or create one of your own using whatever technology is available to you. Remember to apply the principles for good Writing-to-Learn assignments listed on p. 15.

- **E-journals.** English professor Paula Gillespie explains that her electronic journal assignment became the "centerpiece" of her introduction to literature class. Each week students were required to write a "screenful" email about the reading, responding to a prompt designed to guide the discussion and link it with what was happening in class. The whole class had to read all the postings and then respond in another posting. When a particularly good post appeared, Gillespie pointed it out to the group in her own posting.[3]

- **Class summaries.** Education professor Robert Wolffe used email journals in a math class for education majors. Students would email the professor at the end of each class period or once a week, summarizing the information covered in class and sharing questions about the material. Because of the assignment, the students kept up with their reading and learned to ask constructive questions.[4]

- **Extra-credit questions.** Biology professor Deborah Langsam and English professor Kathleen Yancey explain how the professor of an introductory biology course gave extra credit points to students who responded via email to "Biochallenge" questions, which forced the students to apply concepts learned in class to an unfamiliar context. This allowed students to think through the concepts in new ways, and it allowed instructors to respond and ask for expanded answers.[5]

WRITING IN THE DISCIPLINES (LEARNING TO WRITE)

Including writing as an instructional aid will certainly improve students' comprehension of the material, but another important reason to include writing in subject-based classes is that writing is vital to students' professional achievement. Students should learn to write in the classes that prepare them for their future careers. Ask professionals in your field, and they will usually explain that writing is an important part of what they do every day. A research chemist must write an accurate report of her findings. A business executive must write a clear explanation of his marketing plan. An engineer must write a persuasive proposal to receive funding for her project. A doctor must write detailed notes on his cases for insurance purposes. Your future job may involve research, production, or management, but in nearly every situation you must be able to communicate—in *writing*—what you are doing.

Often entirely different kinds of writing, or genres, are required in one discipline than in another, and each genre requires adherence to specific conventions for presentation and documentation. For example, pp. 18–19 feature the introductions from articles in a chemistry journal and in an English composition journal. The differences in the two pieces of writing are immediately evident. The chemistry article uses figures and headings to present and organize material visually, while the English article does not. The English article starts with an almost anecdotal introduction, while the chemistry article moves directly into its main focus. The English article is more personal, leisurely, and literary in tone, while the chemistry article is concise, direct, and objective. Students need to learn these kinds of discipline-specific conventions, and they can best learn them from a practicing professional in the field, such as you.

In addition, each discipline requires different formats for different types of writing: a certain structure for a case study, another structure for a book review, and so on. (See Table 2.1.) These various requirements can be complete mysteries for novices such as your students.

The subject-area classroom is the best place for students to learn to write in these various professional genres because:

■ The professor and you, as experienced subject-area writers, can mentor and guide the student novices to an understanding of appropriate writing conventions.

■ Students read subject-specific writings that serve as professional models for their own writing.

■ Students can practice discipline-appropriate types of writing.

■ As students come to understand the theoretical underpinnings of their discipline, they will understand better how to communicate in that discipline.

The Writing Process

Because writing is important in courses across the curriculum and in the disciplines, both to enhance learning and to teach discipline-specific style and con-

Acc. Chem. Res. **2002,** 35, 19–27

Excited-State Proton Transfer: From Constrained Systems to "Super" Photoacids to Superfast Proton Transfer[†]

LAREN M. TOLBERT* AND KYRIL M. SOLNTSEV
School of Chemistry and Biochemistry, Georgia Institute of Technology, Atlanta, Georgia 30332-0400

Received March 29, 2001

ABSTRACT
We have used knowledge of the electronic structure of excited states of acids to design molecules that exhibit enhanced excited-state acidity. Such "super" photoacids are the strongest photoacids known and allow the time evolution of proton transfer to be examined in a wide array of organic solvents. This includes breaking/formation of the hydrogen bonds in hundreds of femtoseconds, solvent reorientation and relaxation in picoseconds, proton dissociation, and, finally, diffusion and geminate recombination of the dissociated proton, observed in nanoseconds.

General Principles

Simple thermodynamics for the ground and excited states of any proton-containing molecule (AH) and its conjugate base predict that its excited state (*AH) is a stronger acid than the ground state if the absorption or emission spectrum of the conjugate base is characterized by a bathochromic shift relative to that of the conjugate acid ($hv_1 > hv_2$, see Figure 1).[1] This thermodynamic cycle is described by the Förster equation, eq 1,[2] where $pK_a^* =$

$$pK_a^* = pK_a - (hv_1 - hv_2)/2.3RT \qquad (1)$$

$\Delta G_a^*/2.3RT$ is the ground (excited)-state acidity constant and $hv_{1(2)}$ is the energy of the 0−0 electronic transition for the conjugate acid (base). In this scheme, k^*_{pt} and k^*_{-pt} are the rates for forward and back excited-state proton transfer, respectively, $k_f(')$ and $k_{nr}(')$ are rates of acid (base) fluorescence and nonradiative decay, and $k_q(')$ is the rate of acid (base) quenching by protons. A more general and useful treatment is to take v_1 and v_2 as the averages of the absorption and fluorescence transitions of each acid and base species.

Laren M. Tolbert received his Ph.D. in 1975 with Howard Zimmerman at the University of Wisconsin and was a postdoctoral fellow with R. B. Woodward at Harvard University during 1975–1976. He has been at Georgia Tech since 1985, where he is currently Professor and Chair of the School of Chemistry and Biochemistry and Associate Editor for the *Journal of the American Chemical Society.* He is a Fellow of the American Association for the Advancement of Science.

Kyril M. Solntsev was born in Moscow in 1969. He received his M.Sc. (1991) and Ph.D. (1996) degrees from the Department of Chemistry, Moscow State University (Prof. Michael G. Kuz'min). During his joint postdoc at Hebrew University (Prof. Noam Agmon) and Tel-Aviv University (Prof. Dan Huppert), he studied diffusional kinetics of the excited-state proton transfer of "super" photoacids. He is currently a postdoctoral fellow at Georgia Tech.

10.1021/ar990109f CCC: $22.00
Published on Web 11/27/2001

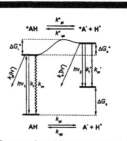

FIGURE 1. Proton transfer and decay processes in photoacids.

Since $pK_a^* = -\log_{10}(k^*_{pt}/k^*_{-pt})$, the pK_a^* obtained from the Förster calculation, referred to here as the Förster acidity, must be considered an approximation. Another approach uses fluorescence titration, in which the emissions from the conjugate acid and base are examined as a function of pH.[3]

Molecules that undergo significant colorization upon deprotonation, e.g., triarylmethane dyes, should thus be powerful proton donors. For instance, 9-phenylfluorene[4] has a predicted pK_a^* of −13! The conjugate bases of such systems are often resonance-stabilized carbanions, and their bathochromic shifts result from the generation of an n→π* absorption.[4] Regrettably, such thermodynamic acidity has not been evinced in spontaneous deprotonation of photoexcited hydrocarbons to yield excited-state carbanions, although Wan has developed several compelling suggestions of their intermediacy.[5] Despite the predicted acidity, the protolytic photodissociation of 9-phenylfluorene is not observed, because the C−H bond breaks too slowly to establish equilibrium within the lifetime of the excited state. The relevant parameters are inevitably rates, not driving force. Nevertheless, thermodynamics can still be a powerful guide to the choice of appropriate systems.

In contrast to hydrocarbon photoacids, many hydroxyarenes (AH ≡ ArOH) exhibit proton transfer competitive with excited-state decay. The hydroxyarenes have fluorescent conjugate bases with nonbonding oxygen-centered molecular orbitals and excited states with charge distribution at sites distal from oxygen. This reduces the basicity of the excited-state anion and, by analogy, increases the acidity of the conjugate acid. This is equivalent to Weller's "intramolecular charge transfer" rationalization of the acidity in photoexcited hydroxyarenes.[2]

Hydroxyarenes undergo a number of processes in addition to fluorescence and excited-state proton transfer (ESPT), shown in Figure 1. These include various nonradiative processes characteristic of hydroxyarenes such as proton-induced quenching and homolytic OH bond cleavage to produce radicals, studied most extensively for

[†] Dedicated to the memory of G. Wilse Robinson, Georgia Outstanding Alumnus, and lifelong contributor to the field of proton transfer.

Article 2.1.

Clearing the Air: WAC Myths and Realities

Susan McLeod and Elaine Maimon

Between the two of us, we have accumulated more than forty years of experience in writing across the curriculum. As pioneers in the field, we know the WAC territory because we have explored and helped to map it inch by inch, planting flags on behalf of students and their need both to write to learn and to learn to write. We know the field. So when we heard a featured speaker at a recent WPA conference define WAC in a way that neither of us recognized—reifying false dichotomies and serious misunderstandings—we decided it was time to expose the myths surrounding WAC, to clear the air, to set the record straight.

Comparing notes after the talk, we concluded that what bothered us most was the fact that an informed and respected colleague clearly had in his head an inaccurate map of terrain that both of us knew so well. He referred to formalist concerns with "grammar across the curriculum" and to irreconcilable dichotomies between writing in the disciplines (WID) and writing across the curriculum (WAC). Our simultaneous and shared discomfort at this conference presentation illustrated for us the need to re-historicize WAC and to reposition WAC theory. Our goal is a more enlightened discussion of what WAC is, what it does, and what it can become. This

Susan McLeod is Professor of English and Chair of the English Department at Washington State University, where she also directs writing-across-the-curriculum faculty seminars and teaches graduate and undergraduate courses. As a long-time member of the Board of Consultants of the National Network of Writing Across the Curriculum, she has consulted and led faculty seminars at colleges and universities across the country. She has published articles and books on WAC and writing program administration; her current project is a co-edited collection tentatively titled *WAC for the New Millennium* (forthcoming from NCTE). **Elaine P. Maimon** is Provost (Chief Operating Officer) and Professor of English at Arizona State University West. In the early 1970s, she initiated and then directed the Beaver College writing-across-the-curriculum program, one of the first WAC programs in the nation. She was a founding Executive Board member of the National Council of Writing Program Administrators (WPA). She has co-authored three books and has directed NEH-sponsored national institutes to improve the teaching of writing. Her current project is a spiral-bound freshman composition handbook, co-authored with Janice Peritz (forthcoming from McGraw Hill in 2001).

Article 2.2.

TABLE 2.1.
Specialized Kinds of Writing Common to a Few Disciplines

History	*Physics*	*Sociology*	*Music*
Book review	Lab notebook	Observation	Reaction paper
Research paper	Grant proposal	Interview	Concert review
Narrative	Research article	Case study	Music analysis
Prospectus	Abstract	Experimental report	Program notes

ventions, you may be thinking, "How do I go about teaching writing?" This is obviously a complex question. A good starting place is realizing that writing is a process. Many studies have shown that both professional and student writers follow the same kind of general process to produce written documents. Hardly anything that is written well was written in one draft. If you think back on how you write when you want to write well, you will probably recognize that you follow a process something like the following.

- **Prewriting.** First you think about the subject and contemplate the assignment's purpose, audience, context, scope, style, and format. You mull over ideas for potential topics as you walk, wait at stop lights, shower, or doodle in your notebook. You think about a basic structure for the piece. All of this happens over time, either consciously or subconsciously, either in your head or in writing. Depending on the assignment, you may do research, in either the library or the lab. This is a time when you look for issues, problems, or uncertainties that you think would be interesting to explore (or easy to write about).

- **Drafting.** When you feel ready (or when the deadline starts to loom) you start writing your ideas in sentences and paragraphs. As you work on the draft you will come to understand your subject more clearly, and your focus and structure may shift in subtle or even grand ways. You will begin to formalize your central purpose and structure, formulating a controlling thesis statement. As you try to express your ideas logically and compellingly, you may see that you need more data and will have to return to your research. As you follow a certain line of reasoning, you may discover that it doesn't really work and that you need to find another plan of development. Drafting is the messiest part of the process and perhaps the hardest work of all.

- **Revising.** After you have a pretty good draft, you start to revise. Usually you are so close to the work by this point that it is hard for you to look at it realistically. You may enlist some outside eyes—a friend, a roommate, family member, classmate, writing tutor, TA, or professor—to read over the paper and tell you what is confusing and what needs more evidence. With this feedback, you may make major changes to your draft, changing focus, structure, order, and paragraphs to make your meaning clearer. You may even rewrite the paper.

- **Editing.** Once the draft says pretty much what you want it to, and says it clearly, you probably go through it again to make sure that everything is correct. You may run your computer's spell checker and grammar checker. You may read the paper aloud, looking for errors that the computer tools missed. You may smooth out awkward phrasing and make sure that the punctuation is correct. You may fiddle with the format, putting in headings and page numbers.

■ **Publishing.** Publishing means "making public." As a student, you probably publish most of your work by submitting it to be evaluated by the professor or TA. However, you may also sometimes have the satisfaction of submitting your work to be published to a wider audience, perhaps at a symposium, conference, or even a professional journal. In those cases, you may go over your writing again with a "fine-toothed comb" just to make sure you've caught all your errors and that everything you've written makes sense.

Prewriting, drafting, revising, editing, and publishing. These steps comprise what is called *the writing process.* Of course, the five steps are not really that separate, for the writing process is recursive in nature. (See Figure 2.1; notice how each step encompasses elements of other steps, from prewriting through publishing.) You might return to prewriting-type work in the midst of drafting or even do some editing. Of course, revision is going on all the time, at every step. You do not "finish" one step before you move to the next, and sometimes you "finish" the project only when a deadline forces completion upon you. You can help your students to become better writers by teaching them the steps of the writing process and the strategies for working at each step.

Conclusion

Students need to recognize that writing is a part of thinking, learning, and the work they will do beyond their undergraduate careers. You can help students use the writing process to think through their ideas as they write, to formulate the problems they respond to, and to examine their reasoning and support. One of the leading WAC pioneers, Barbara Walvoord, explains that we "help students

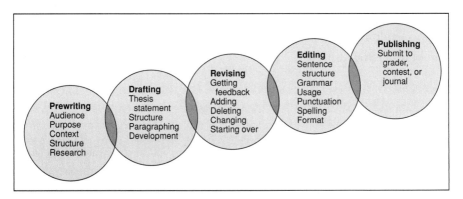

Figure 2.1. The Writing Process

improve writing *as they learn* and *in order to learn* their sociology, biology, business, law, or engineering."[6] Writing is not a separate task in a subject-based classroom. It is a part of the learning that must be done.

Chapter Checklist

☐ Research shows that writing assignments and writing instruction belong in subject-based classes, or across the curriculum.

☐ Short in-class or out-of-class writing assignments enhance learning because writing requires personal involvement and synthesis.

☐ Students in all disciplines need to learn the types of writing specific to their field and the writing conventions that are expected of them as professionals.

☐ Teaching students how to use the writing process in a subject-area class will help them to write better, learn the subject matter more thoroughly, and prepare them to write professionally.

Applications to Your Own Situation

1. Write about a Writing-to-Learn assignment (such as keeping a journal or doing in-class writing) you have completed for a class. How did the assignment help you learn? If you did not find it useful, consider ways to revise the assignment to improve its effectiveness.

2. Following the guidelines in this chapter, think of a brief Writing-to-Learn assignment that would be appropriate for the class you are TAing. Write an explanation of what you hope the assignment will teach students. Refer to the examples on pp. 11–12.

3. Find some good examples of writing in your discipline. Determine the genre of each example. Is it a proposal, a report, a research article, or something else? List some conventions of good writing that are distinctive to your discipline, referring to the models you've gathered. You could turn this into a Writing-to-Learn assignment by having your students complete this analysis themselves.

4. Ask a professional in your field about the role of writing in his or her daily work. Share with your students what you learned about "real world" writing in your field.

5. Write a paragraph describing the process you follow when you write a major paper. Identify the strategies you use while prewriting, drafting, revising, and editing.

Working with Your Professor

1. Discuss with your professor ways to use writing to enhance learning. Together, think of brief Writing-to-Learn assignments that you could incorporate into the class.

2. Look together at the major writing assignments for the class. How do the assignments prepare students to write in your particular discipline? Are there ways to improve the students' preparation for writing in this discipline?

3. Look over your syllabus. Are there any intermediate, sequenced assignments that encourage the students to start the writing process early? (For example, assignments that require students to submit the topic for their paper, then a preliminary bibliography, then a draft for peer review.) Discuss including sequenced assignments, if there are none already scheduled, to discourage students from procrastinating. Such assignments also provide you with an opportunity to comment on the students' writing at multiple points in their writing processes.

CHAPTER 3

Prewriting

"Writing is just having a sheet of paper, a pen,
and not a shadow of an idea of what you're going to say."
—Francoise Sagan

In this chapter you will learn

- how to explain writing assignments by analyzing them for purpose, audience, context, scope, style, and format.
- how to use detailed assignment instructions and grading rubrics to help students write sooner and better.
- how students can use invention strategies to find and focus their topics.
- how to coach students' research and reading skills.

Students confronted with a writing assignment may feel frightened of starting or unsure of what is expected of them, and they will sometimes put off writing until just before their papers are due. When this happens, usually you and your professor have to read poorly written papers, and students learn little more than how much Coke they can drink at 2 A.M.

To prevent procrastination and anxiety, you must get students started on their writing assignments early. They need time to think carefully about the assignment; find interesting questions to explore; conduct research, if necessary; and plan, draft, revise, and edit their papers. This chapter discusses methods you can use to get students started on their assignments—the prewriting step of the writing process.

Explaining Writing Assignments

The first thing you should do is make sure your students understand the writing assignment you are giving them. In order to do this, be sure you understand the assignment yourself. Read the written instructions carefully and review them with your professor, clarifying any questions you may have. Remember: If something isn't clear to you, it probably isn't clear to your students either.

THE FAR SIDE® By GARY LARSON

© 1994 FarWorks, Inc. All Rights Reserved/Dist. by Creators Syndicate

Put a gorilla brain in a cow's head.
Switch Mr. Rodgers brain with a maniac's
Take my cousin's brain inject it with
the DNA from a wolverine, and toss.
Build a giant robot, install som
serrated mandibles on the end of
Take a giant squid and cross

The Far Side® by Gary Larson © 1994 FarWorks, Inc. All Rights Reserved. Used with permission.

The curse of mad scientist's block

The following is a sample writing prompt from an introductory political science class.[i]

Discuss your own political culture. What are your major values and assumptions? In what ways were you socialized? Have changing situations forced you to reevaluate and rework your childhood assumptions? Papers should be five to six pages in length.

The following questions and commentary analyze the preceding assignment. Such an analysis is key to making any writing task as clear and workable for students as possible.

---

[i]Thanks to Donna Lee Bowen, Department of Political Science, Brigham Young University (BYU).

- **What is the purpose?** What does the professor want the students to learn or discover as they write their papers? Perhaps the professor wants the students to reflect on their political background. Perhaps he or she wants them to apply certain terms they have been studying (such as *political culture* and *socialization*) to their own individual situation to demonstrate an internalizing of the concepts. Discuss the professor's motivations with him or her so that you can give your students appropriate guidance.

- **Who is the audience?** You may say, "Obviously the professor." But is it? Usually it is good to think of an audience beyond just the person who will be grading the paper. Students who think they don't have to explain things "because the professor knows it already" forget that the professor wants to know if the students *themselves* understand the material. Ask the professor what kind of audience he or she wants the students to have in mind when they are undertaking a writing assignment.

- **How does the context influence the assignment?** The assignment should also be considered in terms of its context. Because it is part of an introductory political science class, this particular assignment would prompt certain kinds of content, such as detailed explanations of kinds of political cultures. A similar assignment for a sociology class might require different treatment. Students need to think of the assignment in terms of what they have been learning in class.

- **What is the scope of the assignment?** Does the professor want the students to cover *all* their major values and assumptions or limit their discussion to just a few? Does the professor want a complete life history from childhood until the present time or just one or two formative experiences or circumstances? Answers to such questions will make the writing task more specific by helping students zero in on what it is they have to write about.

- **What style is appropriate?** Does the professor want the students to stay with a more formal, scholarly style, or would a personal style (using first person, using descriptive language, etc.) be more appropriate for this assignment? It's quite possible that the professor might have different styles in mind for different types of assignments.

- **What format is expected for the assignment?** This assignment gives a page requirement, but what about font size, margins, line spacing, or headings? Does the professor expect documentation? What style guide is preferred? These details may sound picky, but you should know exactly what the professor has in mind.

Using questions of purpose, audience, context, scope, style, and format to analyze a writing assignment will help you understand what is expected of your students and will also help your students understand what you expect of them. If you are unable to answer any of these questions definitively, you should discuss your concerns with your professor.

Teaching Tip: Discipline-Specific Formats

Students are understandably confused when asked to write in a format that is new to them. Someone who has written only literary analyses for English classes will probably feel somewhat lost when asked to write a lab report for a microbiology class. When a writing assignment requires conforming to discipline-specific conventions your students may not be familiar with, help them understand the expectations. Bring in samples of various successful documents written by both professionals and students to help them visualize the final product. Analyze the documents together in terms of purpose, audience, context, scope, style, and format. You could show the models on an overhead projector during class, make them available on a Web site, or divide the students into groups where they could examine print copies of the models together. Help the students understand what is expected in this kind of writing, and they will feel more capable of meeting those expectations.

Using Detailed Assignment Instructions and Grading Rubrics

After you discuss your analysis of the writing assignment with your professor, he or she might be interested in revising the assignment's instructions. Or, with your professor's guidance, you may choose to create a handout explaining the assignment in more detail. In either case, you and your professor should remember to include specific guidance on purpose, audience, context, scope, style, format, and any other important aspects of the paper. (For example, if your students are writing a scientific report, you might list the individual parts or sections that must be included: Introduction, Methods, Results, Discussion, and Conclusion.) If you decide to prepare a handout, think about what problems the students are likely to have with the assignment and address those problems directly. Clarifying writing assignments will not only help students understand and fulfill the requirements of the assignment, it will also make evaluating the papers much easier once they are written.

Giving students a scoring guide or grading rubric that lists the criteria you or your professor will use to evaluate students' papers is also a good idea. If the students know from the outset what "counts," they will be able to put their energy into meeting those expectations. Example 3.1 features an assignment from a computer science class with instructions and the grading rubric the professor used to evaluate students' papers. (See Chapter 11 or <bedfordstmartins.com /ta_guide> for additional examples of grading rubrics.)

Distributing detailed assignment instructions to your students, and perhaps including a grading rubric, will help them get started on their writing. However, instructions and rubrics should not overcontrol the content of the piece. Assignments that prescribe exactly what to say in each paragraph of the paper do not give students any freedom to explore or discover. A good assignment provides the purpose and guidelines for writing without dictating exactly what to say.

EXAMPLE 3.1. A Writing Assignment and Grading Rubric[ii]

CS 236—FORMAL WRITTEN REPORT

Purpose

The purpose of this assignment is to compare the time to execute two equivalent relational algebra expressions and to explain the results of the experiment to the reader.

Context

You have written a Relational Database System in projects 1 and 2. Your system allows you to execute select, project, and join operations on relations. You have studied relational algebra expressions and you learned that expressions can be optimized. The order of operations in the expression can be changed so that the expression executes in less time but still gives the same result.

Experiment

The following two relational algebra expressions are equivalent. The second expression is an optimized version of the first.

$$\pi_{AD} \left(\sigma_{A=25} \left(\sigma_{E=113} \left(r1 \bowtie r2 \right) \right) \right)$$

$$\pi_{AD} \left(\left(\sigma_{A=25} \, r1 \right) \bowtie \left(\sigma_{E=113} \, r2 \right) \right)$$

Execute each of the relational algebra expressions. Count the number of times a tuple is accessed during execution. The contents of relations r1 and r2 are given by files r1.txt and r2.txt. Relation r1 has scheme ABC and r2 has scheme CDE.

Report

Write a report with the following organization:

- Introduction
- Methods
- Results
- Analysis
- Conclusion

The Methods section tells the reader how you did the experiment. You should give enough information to allow the experiment to be repeated.

The Results section presents your results to the reader. You should present the results in a way that the reader can easily understand the

---

[ii]Thanks to Cory Barker, Department of Computer Science, BYU.

meaning of the results. You may want to use charts or tables. Remember to give units for any numeric values.

The Analysis section explains what the results mean. Help the reader understand the implications of the results. Explain why the two queries have different access counts.

Format

The paper must be typewritten with double-spaced paragraphs, using a 12-point serif font and 1-inch margins.

Grading

The paper will be evaluated using the five criteria listed below. The paper will be judged to be either strong, average, or weak in each area.

Content	Are your ideas accurate, complete, relevant?
Organization	Is the information organized efficiently?
Language	Is the language clear and direct?
Mechanics	Do you use correct spelling, punctuation, grammar?
Format	Is the format easy to access and attractive?

Helping Students Find and Focus Their Topics

When students understand the assignment, they will be better prepared to think about the particular topic they will address in their writing. However, choosing an appropriate topic is always difficult. A good topic for a paper needs to be appropriate to the assignment, sufficiently limited for the scope of the paper, and, above all, interesting to the writer. If the writer is not interested in the topic, no doubt readers won't be either.

Good writers find a good topic by recognizing inconsistencies, problems, or concerns that would bear examination. Linda Flowers and John Hayes, pioneering researchers on the writing process, point out that in many ways writers "create the problems" they intend to solve through writing.[1] As a TA, you can guide your students to find good topics for their writing by giving them exercises that encourage them to think about ideas in fresh ways. Following are prewriting strategies you can use in class or in one-on-one meetings to help your students find topics to write about.

LISTING

After reviewing the assignment instructions with the class, lead a discussion in which students call out possible ways of approaching the assignment while you write the ideas on the chalkboard or a transparency. The rule is that no idea is stupid. Let one idea lead to another. After five or ten minutes of listing, stop and have students write down ideas for their own papers.

Students might come up with the following list for the political science assignment on p. 25:

Republican, Independent, or Democrat?
my stance on "big issues"—political or apolitical?
examples
social institutions
　　— family (mom, dad, grandparents, sisters)
　　— school(s) (friends, teachers, classmates)
　　— neighborhood
　　— religion
　　— geographic region (?)
　　— clubs/teams
experience (direct and indirect)
youth = idealism (innocence)
age = cynicism (experience)

FREEWRITING

The goal here is to get the brain to churn out ideas with the internal editor turned off. For five or ten minutes, as quickly as possible, have the students write everything they can think of in connection with the assignment. Anything goes. They don't even need to write in complete sentences, worry about spelling, or think about grammar. The only restriction is that what they write must have something to do (however slightly) with the assigned paper. Most students will be surprised at what they discover they have to write about.

A student might freewrite the following paragraph in preparation for the Physical Science 100 research paper in Example 12.1 on pp. 121–122.

> We have to write on one of the four physical sciences we have covered. I really liked the astronomy section. I love Star Trek! I would like to see if manned space travel is really a possibility outside of our solar system. Maybe I could find out what would be the physical challenges to that really happening. I read that book Physics of Star Trek—maybe I could start with that and then find some more information in other places. I guess time is an issue. The speed of light and all that. Maybe I could find why we could or couldn't really travel at warp speed some day.

Another idea is to give the students a few minutes to freewrite on each of an assignment's subtopics. For example, for the political science assignment on p. 25, the students could write for three minutes on political culture, two minutes on major values and assumptions, two minutes on how they were socialized, two minutes on how changing situations have influenced them, and so forth. This will help the students look at the assignment from various angles.

CLUSTERING

Clustering (also called webbing or mapping) helps students move from a general idea to a more focused topic for a paper. It has the added benefit of leading to a

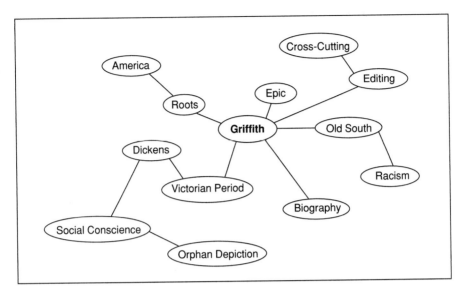

Figure 3.1. Example of a Cluster[iii]

kind of structure for the paper as well. Have students put the main idea for the paper in a circle in the middle of the page. Then draw lines out from the center to various possible subheadings, and then lines from those subheadings to the next possible level.

In a film class, students were asked to write a research paper on an issue in film history. Starting with an interest in the director D. W. Griffith, the cluster in Figure 3.1 could be generated.

The student who prepared the cluster in Figure 3.1 would begin to think of connections he or she may not have made otherwise, moving from Griffith to the Victorian period to Charles Dickens to social conscience to orphan depiction. At some point, the student would find a question or issue that seemed both interesting and focused enough to explore in this particular paper.

The student could then put his or her focused topic in the center of a new cluster to explore ways of developing that idea. For example, the student who completed the cluster in Figure 3.1 might start a new cluster with "Griffith's Depiction of Orphans" in the center, and then explore various possible subsets of that idea.

TALKING

Sometimes just talking is the best way to get the ideas flowing. Try "pair shares." Have the students choose partners to talk with. Explain that one is the talker and the other is the listener. The listener needs to keep the talker talking about his or her paper for a set period of time (maybe five or ten minutes). The listener does

[iii]Thanks to Darl Larsen, Department of Theatre and Media Arts, BYU.

this by acting interested, asking good questions, and being encouraging. Then the students switch roles, and the same procedure is followed. After the talking exercise, have the students write down the ideas they thought of as they talked.[iv]

As a TA you will frequently use the pair-share technique to help students think about their writing. When students come to you for help, encourage them to talk to you about their ideas. Think of good questions to get students talking. Be truly interested in what they say. (For more on conducting one-on-one writing conferences, see Chapter 8.)

WRITING-TO-LEARN ASSIGNMENTS AS INVENTION

Many of the Writing-to-Learn assignments discussed in Chapter 2 could serve as invention exercises for a long paper.

The following are some examples of brief in-class writing prompts or journal assignments. Taking even a few minutes to write answers to questions such as these will help students make real progress toward writing a draft.

- "What do you think you might write your paper on?"

- "What kind of personal experience do you have with the topic we are discussing?"

- "Tell me about one source you have found for your paper."

- "Imagine you are someone who disagrees with your assertions. What arguments would such a person make against your ideas?"

Technology Tactics

Email messages can be an efficient means of preventing procrastination and encouraging prewriting. Try one of the following assignments or create one of your own using whatever technology is available to you. Remember to apply the principles for invention strategies listed on pp. 29–31.

- **Electronic submissions.** Your students can use email to submit their potential topics, thesis statements, or outlines to you. Then you can respond to them in a reply email. This way the students get immediate feedback, and you don't have to take time in class to collect or return anything.

- **Electronic questions.** Students can use email to ask you (or each other) questions about the assignment, clarify requirements, and discuss ideas for papers.

- **Electronic pair shares.** You could require students to email partners about their plans for the upcoming paper. Students would give each other feedback on the ideas, asking questions to encourage further thought.

[iv]See Karen Spear, *Sharing Writing: Peer Response Groups in English Classes*, in the Bibliography, for useful ideas on this topic.

Coaching Related Skills

Often at the prewriting stage students will need help with other skills which are necessary for writing a good paper.

RESEARCH

If the paper is based on library research, students may need help finding sources in your particular discipline. Your professor may be able to arrange for a subject librarian to show students how to access specialized indexes for your discipline. As a more experienced student who has done this kind of research in the past, you can share your own research process, the kinds of indexes you use, how you develop search terms, and how you manage your research once you've gathered it.

Students also need guidance in evaluating sources. Questions such as the following will help students determine if a source is credible.

- Is the source peer reviewed? (That is, does the journal or publisher require manuscripts to be reviewed by experts before publication?)
- Is the source based on solid research? Is there a substantive list of sources?
- Is it objective in tone?
- Is the author an expert in the field?

Internet research is especially problematic. Explain to students that anyone can create a Web site on any topic, whether or not that person is a credible authority on the topic. Teach students to evaluate Web sites carefully, checking for authority, accuracy, bias, and currency.[2]

If original research (laboratory experiments, surveys, interviews, etc.) is required for the paper, students will need to be guided through that research process carefully. For appropriate disciplinary guidelines, confer with your professor and perhaps consult discipline-specific writing guides such as those listed in the Bibliography.

READING

Once they have found sources, students may then need help understanding the material, which is often written for an audience of experts in the field. Take the time to teach students how to read typical professional writing in your discipline. For example, explaining the format of a scientific paper would help students know what to expect from each section. Show the students how to scan abstracts for useful material and how to find what they need in the results sections. Read an article together in class. Give students in- or out-of-class activities that will train them to read critically. Even a little bit of guidance in how to read professional writing can make this information much more accessible.

Also teach students to read their sources actively by making notes in the margins and asking questions of the text. Tell them to cultivate the art of asking

"Why?" Looking for relationships and inconsistencies among their various sources will lead to insightful revelations. Help them to understand that just because something is in print doesn't mean it is necessarily true. Also help them to understand that all authors, however objective they may seem, write from some kind of bias. Learning to watch for that bias can help students to read actively.

Conclusion

For students, getting started is often the hardest part of writing. Guide your students in this difficult task by helping them to understand the requirements of the assignment and by building prewriting and invention exercises into the class. Teach students to research thoroughly and to read with real inquiry. Doing this will lead to better writing and better learning.

Chapter Checklist

☐ Making sure your students understand the assignment is the first step in prewriting.

☐ Detailed writing assignments and grading rubrics clarify expectations for the students and help to prevent frustration, anxiety, and procrastination.

☐ Listing, freewriting, clustering, talking, and even Writing-to-Learn assignments help students find interesting problems or issues to explore in their writing.

☐ Students will likely need direction in finding and reading authoritative sources. They will especially need guidance in collecting original data if that is part of the assignment.

Applications to Your Own Situation

1. Choose a writing assignment from the class you are TAing. Following the model on pp. 25–26, analyze the assignment for purpose, audience, context, scope, style, and format. Were you able to answer all the questions? Do you have any new questions? If necessary, consider ways of revising the assignment to clarify any confusing points.

2. Practice using the invention strategies described in this chapter to start an assignment for the class you are TAing. Which strategy worked best for you? Think of other activities that would help students get started on this particular writing assignment.

3. Reflect on your own experience as a beginning student in your discipline. What advice on conducting research or reading journal articles in your field do you wish you had been given? Compose a list of research and reading tips for your students. Add to the list as students ask you questions and as more ideas come to mind.

Working with Your Professor

1. Discuss the various aspects of the writing assignments for the class you are TAing. Be sure you and your professor understand the expectations for each assignment in the same way, using the analysis model on pp. 25–26. If you have completed the first item from the "Applications to Your Own Situation" exercise, use your findings as a basis for your discussion.

2. Discuss ways to use invention strategies and Writing-to-Learn assignments to encourage the students to start working on their papers early. You and your professor might also consider requiring such intermediate assignments as a preliminary topic for their paper, then a preliminary bibliography, then a draft for peer review.

3. Ask your professor for advice on guiding students' research and reading. If you have completed Application 3, share your list with your professor. Does your professor have any tips, resources, or ideas for teaching research or reading skills that he or she can share? Add his or her suggestions to your list.

CHAPTER 4

Drafting

"Writing is the hardest work in the world not involving heavy lifting."

—Pete Hamill

In this chapter you will learn

- the importance of having students start their drafts early.
- tips for helping students develop appropriately limited controlling objectives or thesis statements.
- techniques that students can use to refine the organization and structure of their papers.
- how to identify and teach paragraph unity, development, and coherence.

The line between prewriting and drafting is a blurry one: Some students draft as a form of prewriting, and others plan so thoroughly that their plans function almost as drafts. The actual line of demarcation doesn't matter. What does matter, however, is that students write a draft and move toward a document that meets the requirements of the assignment.

This chapter discusses methods you can use to help your students through the drafting step of the writing process—getting their ideas down on paper, developing and refining their controlling objectives or thesis statements, finding appropriate structures, and creating well-unified and fully developed paragraphs.

Getting Ideas Down on Paper

Drafting is like peeling an onion; with each draft a student reveals different aspects of his or her paper, different problems to solve. For example, a first draft might reveal a controlling objective or thesis statement that is too broad; when the student fixes that problem, a subsequent draft might reveal an illogical or confusing structure, a poorly supported argument, or incomplete or poorly developed paragraphs. In short, drafting is the step in the writing process where students do the real heavy-duty work of molding and shaping what will become their final papers.

Remember that drafting's enemy is procrastination, and the best way you can prevent students from procrastinating is to force them to get their ideas, however fragmentary or rough, down on paper where they can be polished and refined later or in subsequent drafts. Remind students that as painful as the experience of drafting is, they will save themselves even *more* pain and frustration by drafting now, not the night before their papers are due.

Teaching Tip: The "Quick and Dirty" Draft

Often, students' first drafts are also their final drafts, which leaves students little or no time to refine their work. To combat such procrastination, discuss with your professor the possibility of requiring a "quick and dirty" draft that forces students to start writing. A good time for this draft is when students have had time to complete most of their research but when there is still plenty of time for revision.

- **Start.** Students gather all their prewriting—invention exercises, rough outlines, all their notes and resources—and sit themselves before their computers. They tell their families and friends to leave them alone for the next three to four hours.

- **Write.** Students keep writing, no matter what. If they come to a place where they worry about their reasoning, they type that worry into their drafts. If they find they need more evidence, they type that need into their drafts. They need to ignore the voices in their head that will likely tell them, "This is a waste of time. You're not ready to write. You're just writing garbage." For this exercise to work, they need to just keep writing, ignoring all distractions.

- **Save.** After finishing their drafts, students save their files on their computers' hard drives and on disks. They also print out hard copies but do not read them.

- **Break.** Students take a break and reward themselves with ice cream, chocolate, a game of basketball, or whatever they want. They use this time to separate themselves mentally and physically from their writing.

- **Review.** Later, students read through their drafts critically to consider what to keep as is and what to continue working on. Usually students are pleasantly surprised by the amount of good material they have written. They find they have a better idea of their focus and content and know what they need to do next to make the paper better.

Developing a Controlling Objective or Thesis Statement

Most writing needs to be controlled by an appropriately limited objective. Argumentative academic essays will be controlled by a thesis statement. A formal scientific research report centers on a specific purpose for investigation. In both cases the paper's focus stems from a question, a problem, some issue. The paper is in essence a response to that problem, a way of answering it.

SCIENCE WRITING

In science writing the purpose is determined by the goals of the document. David Porush, a professor at Rensselaer Polytechnic Institute and author of *A Short Guide to Writing About Science,* suggests the following examples of science-related goals for writing:

- To explain a new concept
- To demonstrate the efficiency of a method that you executed
- To lay out in a clear and logical way the data you measured or captured with an experiment
- To describe the existing research or thinking about a problem

The specific answer to concerns such as these should guide your writing in the sciences. Porush suggests that students post their controlling objectives near their computers or on their desks, where they will see them as they write.[1]

THESIS STATEMENTS

Though some writing (such as science reports) may not have a stated thesis, much academic writing in all disciplines does. A thesis statement is the assertion a student will prove in his or her paper, the student's stance on a particular topic, one that is sufficiently limited for the scope of the paper. The entire paper is predicated by the thesis, and every paragraph presents an aspect of the evidence supporting the major assertion. If a paper has a strong thesis, it is likely to be a strong paper. If it does not have a strong thesis, it cannot be a strong paper.

Novice writers usually need help limiting their theses to an assertion that can be supported in the space allowed by the assignment. Sometimes students choose a broad thesis intentionally. Their thinking is something like this: "I'll never be able to write ten whole pages. I had better write on *all* the causes of the French Revolution so that I'll be sure to have plenty of information to fill up the space." Students who think in this way don't understand that a broad thesis is much harder to research (think of all the sources you would need to read to cover *every* cause of the French Revolution), it is almost impossible to prove, and it is probably not very interesting. Help students to recognize an appropriately limited topic, small enough to research thoroughly and large enough to provide an interesting issue to discuss.

Besides teaching students to limit, or narrow, their thesis statements, teach them to make a claim that requires proof, something with an argumentative edge. If the claim made is obvious, readers will not care to read the paper proving it. A good thesis raises questions, makes the reader think "Why is that true?" or "How will that be proved?" Students might start by making an observation about the topic and then asking "So what?" As they keep asking questions about the topic, eventually they will find an interesting angle to the topic, one readers will want to learn more about.

One way to teach students what you expect in the way of a thesis is to show examples. For a literature class, you might show a series of sample thesis statements and discuss each one in turn.

1. The poem "Pied Beauty" is by Gerard Manley Hopkins.
2. "Pied Beauty" is about God's creations.
3. "Pied Beauty" uses diction, form, and alliteration to discuss the diversity of nature.
4. In "Pied Beauty," Hopkins uses alliteration to unite diverse images, demonstrating the unity inherent within the diversity of God's creations.

Students can readily see that Number 1 is too obvious and that Number 2 is too broad. Number 3 may look good, but with a little guidance students begin to see that it is fairly predictable and still quite broad. Number 4, however, is sufficiently limited so that a short essay could discuss the ideas in depth. Besides, it is not obvious; readers will be interested to see how the writer supports this claim with evidence. There is an argumentative edge to this statement. Students begin to understand the kind of thesis that would be appropriate for a college-level literary analysis, one that would add a fresh perspective to the topic being analyzed.

Another technique for teaching students how to prepare good thesis statements is to provide a simple series of questions, such as those in Table 4.1 for science and history topics. Though somewhat formulaic, these questions can lead to a very specific and well-balanced thesis that students would then revise or simplify before plugging into their papers. This type of exercise can help students understand the precision a good thesis demands.

While students are drafting, look for ways to help them develop and refine their thesis statements. Completing a question-type exercise, such as the one featured in Table 4.1, or having students share their ideas with you or each other are good methods for getting students fully involved with their writing at the drafting stage.

TABLE 4.1.
Using a Series of Questions to Develop Thesis Statements[i]

Questions	Responses for Science Topic	Responses for History Topic
What is your topic?	Effectiveness of cystic fibrosis drugs.	U.S. culpability for not bombing and destroying the Nazi concentration camp at Auschwitz.
What is your stance on the topic? State this as a complete sentence.	Tobramycin is the most efficient drug in treating cystic fibrosis.	The United States could not have effectively targeted and destroyed Auschwitz directly.
Why do you believe this? State your reasons in a "because" clause.	Because it directly kills problem-causing bacteria, is easy to administer, and can be used on small children safely.	Because the United States lacked the technological precision and intelligence necessary to destroy the camp's death houses without also destroying many or most of the Jewish captives.

(continued)

TABLE 4.1. *(continued)*		
Questions	*Responses for Science Topic*	*Responses for History Topic*
Why would someone disagree with this? State the opposing opinion in an "although" clause.	Although drugs like Pulmozyme have the same effects with a different mechanism of decreasing the thickness of lung mucous,	Although the United States possessed sufficient firepower and information to attack Auschwitz's industrial sector,
<u>"Although" clause</u> + **Stance on the topic** + *"Because" clause* = Complete thesis statement (may need to be revised or simplified)	<u>Although drugs like Pulmozyme have the same effects with a different mechanism of decreasing the thickness of lung mucous,</u> **Tobramycin is the most efficient drug in treating cystic fibrosis** *because it directly kills problem-causing bacteria, is easy to administer, and can be used on small children safely.*	<u>Although the United States possessed sufficient firepower and information to attack Auschwitz's industrial sector,</u> **the United States could not have effectively targeted and destroyed Auschwitz directly** *because the United States lacked the technological precision and intelligence necessary to destroy the camp's death houses without also destroying many or most of the Jewish captives.*

¹Thanks to Amanda Alleman and Paul Morrison, Brigham Young University Writing Fellow trainees, for these examples.

Finding an Appropriate Structure

In order to write a draft, students must have some preliminary idea of the structure they will follow. *The Elements of Style*, the classic style text by William Strunk and E.B. White, boldly proclaims, "Choose a suitable design and hold to it."² While Strunk and White make this task sound obvious and easy, it is often very difficult to accomplish. As students are drafting, they may find better ways to structure their papers and may need to make adjustments and start over. Even when students are writing in a genre whose format dictates the overall parts of the document, they may need to rethink the organization within each part.

Often different types of writing require certain structures. The lab report, proposal, and research article, for example, have clearly delineated sections, and the writer's task is to present information clearly in each required section. A science professor explained to me that the first step he takes when he begins to draft a research article is to set up the headings in his document: Introduction, Methods, Results, Discussion, and Conclusion. He then works on filling in the necessary information and ideas for each section.

Other times the student needs to determine what particular structure will work best to support the objective or thesis of his or her paper. Thesis-driven papers must show a clear correlation between the thesis and the overall structure. For example, if the thesis has two main parts, the paper should likewise be divided in two sections. If idea A is addressed first in the thesis, idea A should also be addressed first in the paper. Key words used in the thesis should be repeated as signposts at major transitions in the paper. As students firm up their papers' structures, they will begin to refine their objectives and theses and find more appropriate ways of organizing their ideas.

Personality and learning style will sometimes determine a student's approach to organizing his or her paper. Some students like to lay out a firm objective or thesis and outline carefully before they begin to write a draft. Others will prefer to write a draft, rethink their structure and objective or thesis, and then write another draft. Either way works. Let your students know what the options are so that they can choose the method that seems to work best for them. Recognize that not all your students will use the same writing strategies you do. That's fine, as long as at some point they come up with an effective structure for their papers.

The following are some useful techniques for getting your students engaged with planning their papers' structures. (Note: These techniques might be useful in the prewriting and revising steps of the writing process as well.)

- **Mapping.** Have students draw pictures of their papers' structures, using flowchart-like boxes, trees, or circles such as those shown in Table 4.2.[3] These graphic organizers will help students see how their papers are structured and where they need to make adjustments or changes.

- **Grouping.** On index cards or slips of paper, have students write down all the ideas they want to include in their papers, one idea per card or paper. Then, on a large, uncluttered horizontal surface, have students spread out their cards and group similar ideas together. Students can then start playing around with the overall order of the groupings to determine which group would come first, second, and third and then decide what order would work best within each group. Students can keep manipulating the cards until the order seems to fit their audience and purpose. They can then make an outline from the order they see in the cards.

- **Formal outlining.** Have your student create formal outlines of their drafts, using complete sentences and Roman numerals. Students can then check their outlines to make sure that their drafts are logically arranged and make adjustments, if necessary. (Refer to a writing handbook, such as those listed in the Bibliography, for information on outlining conventions.)

- **Informal outlining.** Have students evaluate their structures by composing an outline of the draft as written. On a separate sheet of paper, have students write out their papers' objective or thesis statement. Then, below that statement, have students list each paragraph's topic sentence. Students can check to see if every topic sentence relates back to the objective or thesis and if there is a logical progression of ideas.

TABLE 4.2.

Examples of Mapping Techniques and Their Applications

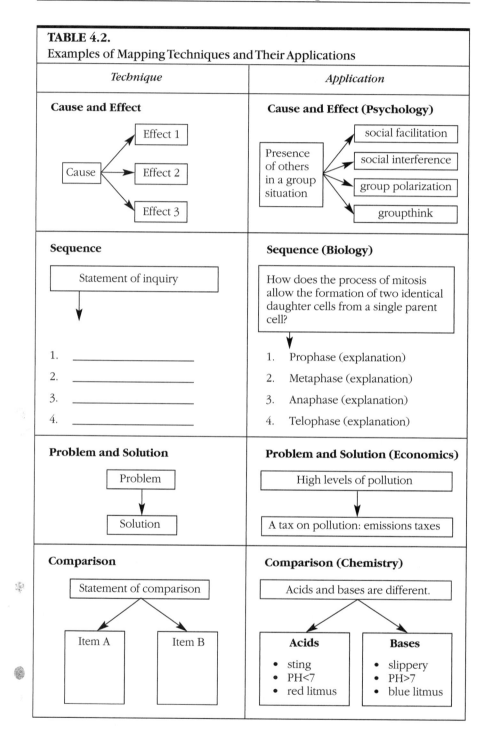

Technique	*Application*
Cause and Effect	**Cause and Effect (Psychology)**
Cause → Effect 1, Effect 2, Effect 3	Presence of others in a group situation → social facilitation, social interference, group polarization, groupthink
Sequence	**Sequence (Biology)**
Statement of inquiry 1. _____ 2. _____ 3. _____ 4. _____	How does the process of mitosis allow the formation of two identical daughter cells from a single parent cell? 1. Prophase (explanation) 2. Metaphase (explanation) 3. Anaphase (explanation) 4. Telophase (explanation)
Problem and Solution	**Problem and Solution (Economics)**
Problem → Solution	High levels of pollution → A tax on pollution: emissions taxes
Comparison	**Comparison (Chemistry)**
Statement of comparison → Item A, Item B	Acids and bases are different. **Acids**: sting, PH<7, red litmus **Bases**: slippery, PH>7, blue litmus

---

Technology Tactics

Using their word-processing programs' drawing tools or a standard art program, such as MS Paint, students can create visual representations, or graphic organizers, of their papers' structures. These electronic representations have the following characteristics.

- **Flexible.** Students can radically change their graphic organizers with a click of the mouse, which makes experimenting with different structural plans easy.

- **Savable.** Students can see how their thinking changes over time by saving each incarnation of their graphic organizers.

- **Recyclable.** Students can copy content from their graphic organizers and paste it into traditional draft documents.

Downloadable graphic organizers, such as those in Table 4.2, are available at <bedfordstmartins.com/ta_guide>. You can distribute copies to your students to complete electronically or in print.

Paragraphing

Paragraphs are the basic unit of writing, the packages determined by subclaims to the main thesis and developed with specific supporting evidence to prove that particular subclaim. Strunk and White elegantly suggest, "A paragraph [should contain] no unnecessary sentences, for the same reason that a drawing should have no unnecessary lines and a machine no unnecessary parts."[4] Within that efficiently composed package, each paragraph needs to be unified, fully developed, and coherent.

UNITY

A topic sentence is the captain of a paragraph: It makes a claim that must be supported by each of the paragraph's sentences. Most well-unified paragraphs follow a simple Claim/Evidence/Comment structure, which accentuates the evidence's support of the claim.

The following paragraph from a human physiology textbook demonstrates the quality of unity.

> In contrast, the sympathetic branch [of the efferent nervous system's autonomic division] is dominant in stressful situations, such as the potential threat from the snake. One of the most dramatic examples of sympathetic action is the fight-or-flight response in which the brain triggers massive simultaneous sympathetic discharge throughout the body. As the body prepares to fight or flee, the heart speeds up; blood vessels to muscles of the arms, legs, and heart dilate; and the liver starts to produce glucose to provide energy for muscle contraction. Digestion becomes a low priority when life and limb are threatened, so blood is diverted from the gastrointestinal tract to skeletal muscles. The massive

sympathetic discharge that occurs in fight-flight situations is mediated through the hypothalamus and is a total body response to a crisis. If you have ever been scared by the squealing of brakes or a sudden sound in the dark, you know how rapidly the nervous system can influence multiple systems of the body.[5]

The following is an analysis of the previous paragraph's structure.

Claim

[T]he sympathetic branch [of the efferent nervous system's autonomic division] is dominant in stressful situations. . . . One of the most dramatic examples of sympathetic action is the fight-or-flight response.

Evidence

1. As the body prepares to fight or flee, the heart speeds up; blood vessels to muscles of the arms, legs, and heart dilate; and the liver starts to produce glucose to provide energy for muscle contraction.
2. Digestion becomes a low priority when life and limb are threatened, so blood is diverted from the gastrointestinal tract to skeletal muscles.
3. The massive sympathetic discharge that occurs in fight-flight situations is mediated through the hypothalamus and is a total body response to a crisis.

Comment

If you have ever been scared by the squealing of brakes or a sudden sound in the dark, you know how rapidly the nervous system can influence multiple systems of the body.

You can easily see how every piece of information in the example paragraph supports the claim that the fight-or-flight response is a powerful example of the function of the sympathetic branch of the autonomic division of the nervous system.

DEVELOPMENT

To convince your audience, you need specific, detailed evidence in support of your claim.

The following is a paragraph from Jared Diamond's Pulitzer Prize–winning anthropology book *Guns, Germs, and Steel: The Fates of Human Societies,* which has been modified to show only abstract support for its claim. Immediately following is the original paragraph, with its specific details underlined.

Paragraph 1: Abstract Support

A stored food surplus built up by taxation can support other full-time specialists besides kings and bureaucrats. This food surplus is very important because it can be used to feed different kinds of workers. Having specialized workers can allow a civilization to grow.

Paragraph 2: Specific Support

A stored food surplus built up by taxation can support other full-time specialists besides kings and bureaucrats. Of most direct relevance to wars of conquest, it can be used to feed <u>professional soldiers. That was the decisive factor in the British Empire's eventual defeat of New Zealand's well-armed indigenous Maori population. While the Maori achieved some stunning temporary victories, they could not maintain an army constantly in the field and were in the end worn down by 18,000 full-time British troops.</u> Stored food can also feed <u>priests, who provide religious justification for wars of conquest; artisans such as metalworkers, who develop swords, guns, and other technologies; and scribes, who preserve far more information than can be remembered accurately.</u>[6]

The first paragraph shown here just says the same thing over and over again, but the second paragraph uses specific details to develop and support its claim. The second paragraph's extended illustration of professional soldiers' importance to Britain's conquest of New Zealand is especially compelling, but the details about priests, metalworkers, and scribes also show why stored food is important. These specific details effectively uphold the paragraph's claim that a "stored food surplus built up by taxation can support other full-time specialists besides kings and bureaucrats."

COHERENCE

The order in which information is presented in a paragraph must be logical, with each sentence connecting the sentences that come before and after it. This quality of connectedness is sometimes called *coherence*. Some ways to provide coherence in a paragraph are to repeat key words, use parallel structure, and provide transitions.

The following is a paragraph, from a business textbook, that demonstrates coherence. *Key words,* <u>parallel structure</u>, and **transitions** are marked to show how they contribute to the paragraph's overall coherence.

Today's factory must *improve* continually to remain competitive in <u>an ever changing and uncertain environment</u>. Factories that <u>expect and encourage</u> *change* have the flexibility to *<u>adapt and improve</u>* <u>their operations</u>. **However**, action must be taken to ensure that *improvements* <u>are incorporated into the daily routine and become a permanent part of the *standardized* procedure</u>. **Otherwise**, the *improvements* will erode quickly, and the *benefits* will be lost. *<u>Improvement</u>* without *<u>standardization</u>* cannot be sustained.[7]

Notice how the idea of improvement is carried through this paragraph by repeating the key words *improve, change, adapt,* and *improvements.* When *standardized* is introduced as an important concept midway through, it is also repeated again in a subsequent sentence. This repetition of key words, together with meaningful use of the transitions *however* and *otherwise,* and good use of parallel structure, makes every sentence connect to the sentences before and after it. The paragraph is coherent because of the use of language in it.

Paragraphs are the basic building blocks of writing. If the paragraphs are unified, fully developed, and coherent, the ideas presented in the document will be clearly communicated. As students draft their papers, help them understand how well-crafted paragraphs build well-crafted papers.

Conclusion

Drafting is a messy, painful, recursive business. In the beginning it's like prewriting, but after several drafts it becomes more like revision. Warn your students that they'll likely struggle with drafting. Tell them to just stay with it, and, if possible, require them to draft well before the paper's due date.

Through drafting and then revising and drafting again, writers move from trying to figure out for themselves what they have to say, to trying to say it in a way that will influence a reader favorably.[8] This awareness of audience is honed as students continue revising.

Chapter Checklist

☐ Getting started is the hardest part of writing. Students will need encouragement and prodding to get their ideas down on paper.

☐ At the drafting step, students need help finding an appropriate controlling idea. They also need to find a suitable structure to support that controlling idea.

☐ Different types of writing dictate different types of structures.

☐ Well-written papers have paragraphs that are unified, fully developed, and coherent.

Applications to Your Own Situation

1. Create a continuum of thesis statements ranging from bad to all right to very good. Using the example on p. 39 as a model, lead a class discussion on identifying appropriately limited thesis statements. Alternatively, use the series of questions in Table 4.1 with your students to draft a sample thesis statement that would be appropriate for a hypothetical paper written for the class you are TAing.
2. Go to <bedfordstmartins.com/ta_guide> and download the graphic organizers that are based on the mapping techniques in Table 4.2. Distribute copies, either electronically or in print, to your students so that they can begin analyzing and improving their papers' structures.
3. Identify a paragraph that exemplifies the qualities of unity, development, and coherence in a piece of writing that is appropriate for your discipline. Make three copies or transparencies of the paragraph (one each for unity, development, and coherence). As modeled on pp. 43–45, use different colored highlighters to show how individual elements work together to create unified, developed, and coherent paragraphs. You could turn this into a Writing-to-Learn assignment by having your students complete this analysis themselves.

Working with Your Professor

1. Discuss requiring students to complete a "quick and dirty" draft. (Refer to the Teaching Tip box on p. 37.) Also, ask your professor if he or she knows of any other methods to encourage drafting or combat procrastination. Discuss how you can incorporate those methods into the class.

2. Discuss the possibility of meeting with your students individually to review their drafts during your office hours. (For information on conducting one-on-one writing conferences, see Chapter 8.)

3. Ask your professor if he or she could suggest good examples of writing in your discipline that display appropriately limited controlling objectives or thesis statements, logical structures, and unified, well-developed, and coherent paragraphs. Use paragraphs from these examples to complete Application 3 with your students.

CHAPTER 5

Revising

*"The beautiful part of writing is that you don't have to get it right
the first time—unlike, say, a brain surgeon."*

—Robert Cromier

In this chapter you will learn

- how to encourage global revision in students' papers.
- how to plan, manage, and conduct effective peer-review sessions.

At some point during the drafting process, students shift from drafting to revising, from simply writing down their ideas to fine-tuning what they have written. Students begin to think less about themselves ("What am I saying?") and more about their readers ("How can I say this as clearly as possible for my audience?").

Revising means "to see again" what has been written, to evaluate one's writing critically for ways to make it better. With this new vision, students can see where they need to add, delete, move, or change things in their papers. This chapter discusses methods you can use to help your students revise on the global level and consider audience feedback to improve their papers.

Global Revision

A student once said, "Revision! Who has time to revise? I never revise because my papers are late as is. I mean you're at the keyboard, you're checking your watch, as you're going [in] like, three minutes to class. . . . It's like writing roulette!"[1] Indeed, many students don't give themselves enough time for substantive revision before they turn in their papers. And even if students do allow themselves time to revise their papers, they usually make only "local" changes to words or sentences. However, most drafts need revision on the "global" level, rethinking the entire world of the piece, not just the surface problems.

Nancy Sommers, director of the Harvard Expository Writing Program, conducted research comparing the revision strategies of student writers and experienced adult writers. Table 5.1 compares student and experienced writers' self-descriptions of their revision processes.[2]

As Table 5.1 shows, student writers in this study had much different ideas of revision from their more experienced counterparts. The students thought that after writing a draft they had only to make surface, or local, changes to their pa-

TABLE 5.1.
Writers' Descriptions of Their Revision Processes

Student Writers	*Experienced Writers*
"I read what I have written and I cross out a word and put another word in."	"It is a matter of looking at the kernel of what I have written, the content, and then thinking about it, responding to it, making decisions, and actually restructuring it."
"I go over it and change words around."	"In one draft, I might cross out three pages, write two, cross out a fourth, rewrite it, and call it a draft. I am constantly writing and rewriting. There are levels and agenda which I have to attend to in each draft."
"I just review every word and make sure that everything is worded right."	"Rewriting means on one level, finding the argument, and on another level, language changes to make the argument more effective."
"The changes that I make are usually just marking out words and putting different ones in."	"My first draft is usually very scattered. In rewriting, I find the line of argument."
"I throw things out and say they are not good. I like to write like Fitzgerald did by inspiration, and if I feel inspired then I don't need to slash and throw much out."	"It means taking apart what I have written and putting it back together again. I ask major theoretical questions of my ideas, respond to those questions, and think of proportion and structure."

pers—to "clean them up." Essentially, they were moving from drafting directly to editing, skipping the revising step of the writing process altogether. The experienced writers, in contrast, saw their drafts as opportunities to reconsider what they were saying and then to find ways to say that more clearly, taking full advantage of the revising step.

Rather than just changing words and sentences, global revision involves fundamental alterations, such as *adding* information, *deleting* unnecessary paragraphs or sentences, *changing* the overall structure, or *moving* sentences, paragraphs, or sections to more appropriate locations. Sometimes at the revising step writers will discover that what they have written is not what they wanted to say after all and decide to start over.

As a TA you can encourage your students to look at their drafts globally, to look critically at their objectives or thesis statements, topic sentences, evidence, overall structure, and paragraphing before they move on to the local level of checking spelling and so forth (in the editing step). You can do this by reading their drafts and commenting on the global issues, either in writing or in one-on-

one meetings during your office hours. (Chapters 8, 10, and 11 provide more detailed information on doing this effectively.) But you can also, with your professor's approval and cooperation, give the students opportunities to respond to each other's drafts in peer-review groups.

Peer-Review Groups

Peer-review groups are a good way to give students another "view" of their writing so that they can revise their papers more effectively. Such peer-review sessions can be very effective for a number of reasons.

- The students reviewing the writing are in the same class and are working on the same assignment. They know the requirements of the assignment and the professor's expectations.

- The students have tried to write the paper themselves and are aware of the difficulties inherent to the assignment.

- Just by reading other people's drafts, the students will come to a better understanding of what is required of them to fulfill the assignment.

But problems are inherent in this situation, too. As the Peanuts cartoon below indicates, it is not easy to give feedback that leads to good revision.

Lucy gives Snoopy what seems to be a thoughtful response and is careful not to take over the author's responsibility. However, she doesn't explain what she means; Snoopy does what she says without thinking for himself, and his revision is much worse than his draft.

The following is a list of things that could go wrong in peer-review sessions.

- **"No. Give me your pen—I'll take care of it."** A "know-it-all" student might try to take over the paper, changing everything and taking away the authority of the writer.

- **"It's a good paper. I—uh—really like it."** A sensitive student might worry about hurting someone's feelings and hesitate to say anything the least bit critical.

- **"You should have only *two* spaces here."** Some reviewers may insist on focusing on local-level errors rather than more global issues of focus, structure, and content.

- **"Oh. Okay . . . I'll make that change right now!"** An insecure writer will implement suggested changes without considering whether they will really work for his or her paper.

- **"Where did you go for spring break last year?"** Distracted students may find it easier to talk about anything other than the papers at hand.

If you and your professor choose to use peer-review groups, you can do some important things to maximize the advantages while minimizing the disadvantages. Students will give more helpful feedback to each other if you and your professor prepare them well by providing clear guidelines, planning and managing the process carefully, and holding students accountable for careful preparation and participation.

Teaching Tip: Listening Skills

Sometimes students may need more direct instruction in truly "listening" to what a student is saying in a paper. Karen Spear, a professor of English who has published extensively on peer review, offers the following ideas for teaching specific listening in a classroom.[3]

- **Attending.** Peer reviewers need to pay attention to what is said (or written). Practice this skill through pair shares, requiring that one of the pair simply listen to the other for five or ten minutes. This keeps students from focusing on what they will say next rather than on what their partner is saying. (See p. 31 for more information on pair shares.)

- **Reflecting.** Reviewers learn to say back to writers what they think has been said. Then writers can see if they have communicated what they wanted to. You can have class exercises in paraphrasing what another person has said.

- **Connecting.** Reviewers should be able to summarize the main ideas of the paper and make connections between the various ideas. You can practice these skills in class if you stop a discussion once in a while and ask a student to summarize what has been said or compare what student A said to the comments of student B.

PROVIDE GUIDELINES

General guidelines such as the following should guide all peer-review sessions.

- **The author is in charge.** No one can take responsibility for the paper away from the author. The author solicits feedback and guides the discussion of his or her paper, and the author makes final decisions about how to revise it. Tell the students that the author must initiate the discussion of his or her paper.

- **This draft is a work in progress.** Everyone must understand that the draft under consideration is not finished. The author knows that the draft needs revision. He or she is looking for help in making decisions about changes to make. Most students are very nervous at first about sharing their writing. The first time we do peer review, I usually have the whole class recite in unison, "This is a really lousy draft." After making this group admission, everyone laughs in relief and we can get on with the review.

- **Be both supportive and challenging.** Suggest that each discussion of a paper begin with specific positive feedback ("The support in paragraph 7 is terrific. I'm convinced."). Then the group should move on to specific challenging comments and questions ("I don't understand the connection between parts 2 and 3. What kind of a transition would make that connection clear to the reader?").

- **Be specific.** Neither supporting nor challenging feedback is helpful unless it is very specifically worded. Teach students to point to specific places in the paper rather than discussing the paper as a whole.

For each peer-review session, the professor and you could provide a list of questions to help guide students' discussions on each others' drafts and further highlight the expectations for the writing assignment itself. Example 5.1 features a peer-review form for a geology term paper. Example 5.2 features a peer-review form for an international nutrition report.

EXAMPLE 5.1.   Peer-Review Form for a Geology Term Paper[i]

GEOL 111—PEER-REVIEW FORM
Title of paper: _____
Author of paper: _____
Peer reviewer: _____
1. Is the title of the paper appropriate?
2. To what extent has the stated purpose been met?
3. Are the basic data presented clearly and in a logical form?

---

[i]Thanks to Eric Christiansen, Department of Geology, Brigham Young University (BYU).

4. Are the illustrations clear, relevant, and well prepared? Are additional illustrations needed?

5. Are the facts separated clearly from the interpretations?

6. Is the paper well organized?

7. Is the paper written clearly?

8. Are the conclusions supported by the data presented? (Most important)

9. Are all the references cited in the text included in the References Cited section at the end of the paper?

EXAMPLE 5.2. Peer-Review Form for an International Nutrition Report[ii]

NDFS 380—PEER-REVIEW FORM

Use this form to evaluate the technical reports of your peers from the task force. The general secretary will be using the same criteria to evaluate the final versions of the reports and proposals. In your comments address what was well done, anything that was unclear or inadequately supported, and suggestions for improvement.

5 – Excellent
4 – Good
3 – Adequate
2 – Needs improvement
1 – Poor or not present

Criterion	Rating	Comments
Technical accuracy		
Main ideas clearly stated		

(continued)

[ii]Thanks to Alison Lemon, Department of Nutrition, Dietetics, and Food Science, BYU.

EXAMPLE 5.2.   *(continued)*

Criterion	Rating	Comments
Arguments and proposals logically and adequately supported		
Questions answered and/or format followed		
Citations and references correct, appropriate, and accurate		
Grammar, spelling, and punctuation correct		
Professional presentation (title, format, language, tone)		

Other comments:

PLAN AND MANAGE THE PROCESS

To be effective, the peer-review process needs to be carefully planned and managed. Together with your professor, consider the assignment, the students, and the time available as you consider the following questions.

- **Should the peer review be oral, written, or online?** Oral reviews are collaborative and give authors and reviewers the opportunity to discuss possible revisions and try out ideas informally. Written reviews allow the reviewers to think carefully about their reactions to the piece and explain their suggestions more thoroughly. Online reviews are written reviews that take place on a class Web site or through email. (See the Technology Tactics box on p. 55.)

- **Should the review take place in class or out of class?** For out-of-class peer review, the students can exchange drafts, respond to them carefully at home, and then return reviewed papers in class. The students could also meet in groups outside of class to discuss their papers, or they could exchange reviews via email. (See the Technology Tactics box on p. 55.)

- **How large should the review groups be?** Groups of three are small enough to allow time to discuss all the papers in a single in-class review session. Also, students get to read more than one draft and get feedback from more than one reviewer. Being able to make comparisons among drafts helps students see what works and what doesn't. If the number of students isn't divisible by three, have one group of four or two groups of two.

- **Should the groups be assigned or self-selected?** There are advantages to both methods. Assigned groups can be arranged so that at least one strong writer is in each group. Self-selected groups usually feel comfortable working together.

- **When should I explain procedures?** However you assign groups, be sure to give all necessary direction *before* dividing up the class. Once students form their groups, they begin to talk and won't hear the rest of your instructions.

- **When is the best time to hold a peer-review session?** Arrange to hold peer-review sessions when students have had time to write a good draft and when there is still time for substantive revision, perhaps after students complete their "quick and dirty" drafts. (See the Teaching Tip box on p. 37.)

Technology Tactics

If you have a class Web site, you can set up online peer-review groups to encourage revision. Students can post their papers to the class's site, select and download a paper to review, and then repost the commented-on paper.

Pamela Flash and Lee-Ann Kastman Breuch of the University of Minnesota researched the advantages and disadvantages of "virtual peer response." Their findings are summarized here.[4]

Advantages of Virtual Peer Response	Disadvantages of Virtual Peer Response
The activity is an exercise in writing rather than speaking, thus encouraging writing practice.	Loss of face-to-face interaction; perhaps less interpersonal interaction in short-term projects.
Students may spend more time reflecting on comments they give to peers, knowing that their comments will be recorded.	Delayed feedback may frustrate some who want immediate feedback.
Students may offer more comments about the global aspect of writing.	Possibly students may offer less feedback on local issues such as grammar or mechanics.
Students may continue their online discussion of writing outside of class because of the convenience.	Student access to technology outside of class may vary.

(continued)

Technology Tactics *(continued)*	
Advantages of Virtual Peer Response	**Disadvantages of Virtual Peer Response**
Students gain exposure to a variety of communication technologies: word processing, email, groupware tools.	Problems with technology (loss of documents, failed attachments) may discourage students.

HOLD STUDENTS ACCOUNTABLE

Students will take the peer-review process seriously if you demonstrate clearly that *you* take it seriously. The following are some suggestions for holding students accountable for their drafts and their contribution to the peer-review process.

- **Require good drafts.** Check students' drafts quickly to make sure they are serious efforts worth subjecting to peer review.

- **Give points.** Reward students for having good drafts and participating constructively in the peer-review session.

- **Move around the room.** If the peer review is held during class, circulate around the room, listen in, answer questions, and keep students on schedule. (This is a good time to check students' drafts and give points.)

- **Reinforce good comments.** Jot down good, constructive comments you hear. After the review session, read these comments back to the class to model the type of feedback students should be giving each other.

- **Assign grades.** Evaluate formal written peer-review comments according to pre-specified criteria.

Conclusion

John Updike said, "Writing and rewriting are a constant search for what it is one is saying."[5] Experienced writers realize that global revision is necessary even after a draft has been written. They depend on the responses of others to know if what they have written is saying what they want it to. As a TA, you can help your students understand the importance of global revision by requiring drafts to be written early enough that there is time for revision. You can also train students to give good peer review to each other's papers. Then your students will come to understand the satisfaction of revising their work. Ellen Goodman, the Pulitzer Prize–winning columnist, explains this satisfaction. "What makes me happy is rewriting. In the first draft, you get your ideas and your theme clear. But the next time through, it's like cleaning house, getting rid of all the junk, getting things in the right order, tightening things up. I like the process of making writing neat."[6]

Chapter Checklist

☐ Revision means to "see again," to look at the draft with a fresh perspective and find ways to make your message clearer to those who read it.

☐ Student writers need to understand the necessity for global revision, large-scale changes of meaning, structure, and support. These more fundamental areas need to be strengthened before moving on to sentence-level editing.

☐ Peer-review groups, if well planned and managed, can teach students to see writing more objectively and to have a better understanding of the craft of good writing.

Applications to Your Own Situation

1. How has revision helped you to rethink what you are saying in a piece of writing? What strategies did you use to "re-see" the piece of writing from the perspective of the reader?

2. Remember a time you participated in a peer-review group. What was helpful about the review? What was not? How could the experience have been managed so that the review would have been more productive?

3. Would a peer-review experience be useful in the class you TA? Following the suggestions on pp. 51–52, make a plan for providing an effective peer-review session in your classroom.

Working with Your Professor

1. Discuss with your professor ways to encourage substantive revision of drafts.

2. Consider with your professor the possibility of using peer-review groups to give the students feedback on their writing. If you completed Application 3, share with your professor ideas for implementing your plan.

CHAPTER 6

Editing

"All morning I worked on the proof of one of my poems, and took out a comma; in the afternoon I put it back."

—Oscar Wilde

In this chapter you will learn

- how to teach students to improve their writing style, including the appropriate use of active or passive voice and specialized language.
- how to make students responsible for correct and effective mechanics, usage, grammar, spelling, and punctuation.

Once the paper says basically what it needs to say with clear focus, structure, and support, students should turn their attention to concerns of style and mechanics. This is not to say that students shouldn't think about such things during the drafting and revision steps. Of course they'll fix a misspelled word when they see it and rephrase a garbled sentence when it is bothersome, but why spend a lot of time changing style in a paragraph that might be deleted before the paper is finished? The time for careful attention to such details is just before submission, and this step *must not be skipped*. The reader of a piece of writing cannot help but be influenced by the clarity of writing *and* the cleanness of mechanics. If these qualities are missing, the student loses credibility, no matter how carefully considered the content of his or her paper is.

As a TA, you probably will not be able to spend much time teaching these skills, but this chapter discusses ways you and your professor can make students aware that clear style and correct mechanics matter in writing, no matter the discipline.

Style

I will not try to provide here a thorough discussion of style. Numerous writing handbooks do that, and entire books have been written on the subject. (See the Bibliography.) Specialized guides to writing in certain disciplines give specific guidelines for discipline-specific style. A few guidelines, however, are applicable to all disciplines and can aid you in helping students improve their writing style.

In whatever discipline you write, good writing is clear writing. The purpose of writing is to communicate; if the language chosen obscures or makes communication difficult, it is not achieving its purpose. In fact, often unclear writing is caused by unclear thinking, or even dishonest intentions. George Orwell said, "The great enemy of clear language is insincerity. When there is a gap between one's real and one's declared aims, one turns, as it were instinctively, to long words and exhausted idioms, like a cuttlefish squirting out ink."[1] When you find students relying on obscure, complex language, work with them to see if they really know what it is they want to say. Once the student's confusion is gone, the awkward style will often disappear as well.

Clear writing is compelling writing. Let your students know that using language that is stuffy, needlessly complex, and hard to understand will not improve their grades. Some students may say that complex language is expected in their field. Some may think that speaking simply and directly will reflect poorly on the quality of their thought. Science writing specialist David Porush responds to this assertion:

> It is easy to believe that pretentious writing is important to how your message will be received. Yet the real basis of your authority as a writer is the work you've performed as a scientist; the research you've done in collecting data, analyzing it, interpreting it, and matching it to current theories or knowledge; and how well your writing explains this work to your audience. . . . [Y]ou can quickly lose your authority as a scientist by undermining your audience's confidence in you as a writer.[2]

Writers in all disciplines need to recognize that clarity of expression allows a reader to understand the quality of the ideas in a document. The language and sentence structure of a piece of writing serves the reader best when it is clear and easy to follow.

Voice

Choosing the appropriate *voice* for a sentence clarifies style almost automatically. If the actor of a sentence is in the subject position, then the sentence is in the *active voice.* (Janice hit the ball into the woods.) If the object of the action is in the subject position, then the sentence is in the *passive voice.* (The ball was hit into the woods by Janice.)

Help your students understand when to use active voice and when to use passive. Writing in the active voice is usually more clear and easy to follow. Sometimes, though, especially in science writing, passive voice better expresses the appropriate emphasis. Explain to your students that, as writers, they must decide which is most clear and effective for their particular situation. (Refer to one of the handbooks listed in the Bibliography for more information on active and passive voice.)

Technology Tactics

Editing tools such as spelling and grammar checkers have become indispensable, although hardly infallible, and you should remind students how to use them carefully. Similarly, the multitude of formatting tools available on word processors today allows students to prepare complicated, professional-looking documents, but you should coach students how to format their papers appropriately for your discipline. The following are some suggestions for using a word processor's editing and formatting tools effectively.

- **Spell check.** Be sure students always use their word processors' spell check function. Warn students not to just automatically click on the first suggestion the spell checker offers, however, because it may not be the right word. Also warn students that spell checkers can't tell whether *there*, *their*, or *they're* or *to, two*, or *too* should be used. Students should proofread carefully to check for errors in the use of homonyms such as these.

- **Grammar check.** Though grammar checkers are improving, they still make some serious mistakes. Encourage students to use the grammar checker as a guide, not a foolproof resource. They should reconsider any sentences the checker highlights and then use their own good sense (and a good writing handbook) to decide what to do with the sentence.

- **Fonts.** Although a vast array of fonts are available, most student papers should be written in a 10- or 12-point standard, proportional, serif font, such as Times New Roman for PC users and Times for Macintosh users. If the format for your field allows for it, boldface or italic can be used sparingly for section headings and subheadings. Students should never use more than two fonts on the same document—even on highly formatted documents, such as résumés.

- **Visuals.** If charts, graphs, maps, or pictures are required for the paper, make sure students understand how to use their computers to produce these visuals and make them look professional. Refer to discipline-specific style guides for instructions on how to label and position visuals in students' papers. (See the Bibliography.)

Specialized Language

Specialized language, or jargon, is common in every field, but using unfamiliar language can sometimes compromise a writer's clarity. The challenge for a student is to know when to use jargon and when a more common word would do just as well—or better. Certainly an important consideration is the assumed audience for the piece of writing. For example, writing for a scholarly journal would warrant using more specialized vocabulary than writing for *Time* magazine. Students should ask themselves whether their readers will be familiar with specialized terminology.

Moving beyond audience considerations, Sharon Friedman and Stephen Steinberg offer some sensible guidelines. Use specialized language under the following circumstances.[3]

- The common language is too ambiguous to be useful in specialized discourse.

- No words exist in the common language that adequately express a new idea or describe a new phenomenon.

- The common language is too concrete to be useful in theoretical analysis.

- The common language is so riddled with value judgments that it thwarts objectivity.

- Compared to common language, jargon is more concise.

Still, students should be encouraged to write using simple, common language as much as possible, relying on jargon only when it is absolutely necessary. Students should be especially careful about using language that they are not sure they understand fully.

Encourage your students to use language that is natural for them and to avoid trying to sound like their textbooks. Simple, clear, direct language will communicate much more plainly their understanding of the subject. When a student's writing or language usage is consistently confused or awkward, encourage the student to say what he or she means aloud. Then have the student try to make the writing as clear as his or her spoken explanation.

Mechanics, Usage, Grammar, Spelling, and Punctuation

As a TA for physics, chemistry, political science, or sociology, you do not have a responsibility to teach mechanics, usage, punctuation, or grammar skills, but you do need to let your students know that you expect them to use such skills well in their writing. All too often, a student who will write mechanically clean papers for an English class will think doing so doesn't matter in another subject because "it's not English." You need to make clear that in every discipline poor mechanics reflect poorly on the writer and that the student is responsible to submit *carefully edited work.*

Encourage your students to use a writing handbook when they begin the editing step of the writing process. While you may not have the time in class to teach specific editing skills in depth, students who refer to a writing handbook will be able to teach themselves the editing skills they need help with.

Teaching Tip: Careful Editing

Convincing students that you are serious about error-free and mechanically clean papers can be difficult. The following suggestions will help you encourage your students to edit their papers carefully and take full advantage of the editing step of the writing process.

(continued)

Teaching Tip (*continued*)

- **Encourage in-class proofreading.** Just before submission, let students proofread each other's papers for surface errors. Have the proofreaders mark suspected errors lightly in pencil, and let the authors fix any mistakes they want to in pen. Be available to answer any questions. This will reinforce that you are serious about expecting mechanically clean work.

- **Mark errors.** Mark errors with a check in the paper's margin. If there are more than a few errors, require the student to correct them and resubmit the paper before you record a final grade. *Do not* go through and fix every error for the student. This takes a lot of your precious time and does not teach the student anything.

- **Consult a writing handbook.** Have access to a good writing handbook so that you can check on usage you think is questionable. Encourage students to use a handbook as they prepare their papers. Model the use of handbooks as you meet with students during your office hours. (See the Bibliography for a list of writing handbooks.)

- **Give "unified" grades.** Don't give students "split grades"—one grade for mechanics and another for content. This implies that the mechanics don't really matter. In reality you really cannot separate content from mechanics: Errors may negatively impact the audience so much that the quality of the content may not even be seen.

Conclusion

As you can, teach students important concepts regarding style, mechanics, and format. But don't give students the impression that *only* correctness matters. The substance of what the paper says is merely served (and served well) by the elegance and correctness of its expression and presentation.

Chapter Checklist

☐ Editing for style and mechanics is the penultimate step of the writing process, but it is nonetheless very important. The perceived credibility of a paper often depends on its style and presentation.

☐ In any discipline, good style is clear and straightforward. Students should use the passive voice only when it is necessary and specialized language only when more common language will not communicate meaning well.

☐ Let students know that correct usage and mechanics are important. At the same time, make clear that good mechanics will not make up for illogical, ill-conceived, or poorly supported writing.

Applications to Your Own Situation

1. Examine the style that is used in a model of good professional writing in your discipline. Is it clear? Does it use passive voice? If so, under what circumstances? How is specialized language used? Use your model in class to illustrate your findings.
2. What is a common error you tend to make in your writing (comma splices, semi-colon usage)? Find a good writing handbook and look up the rules for that problem. Make up three sentences that correctly apply that rule. Share your work with your students, modeling how they too can use a handbook to find and correct errors in their own writing.
3. On one set of papers, mark errors with a check in the papers' margins. Evaluate how well this works for your purposes with your students. (See the Teaching Tip box on pp. 61–62.)

Working with Your Professor

1. Discuss the kind of style that is appropriate for the writing produced in the class you are TAing. Ask your professor if he or she has any models of the type of style he or she expects. If so, use one of your professor's models for Application 1.
2. Does your professor prefer active or passive voice? Specialized or common language? Determine what your professor expects and convey that to your students.
3. Together with your professor, determine a policy for dealing with errors in student writing, including how to mark errors on papers and the extent to which errors will affect students' grades. Include these policies in the assignment's instruction sheet and/or grading rubric.

CHAPTER 7

Publishing

"Either write something worth reading or do something worth writing."

—Benjamin Franklin

In this chapter you will learn

- how publication helps students want to write better.
- ways to make students' writing public in the classroom and beyond.

Publishing means "making public." In a sense students do this whenever they submit their work to a grader who will respond to it and judge it, but writing for an audience of one has many limitations. The real reason for writing should be to communicate, not to get a grade. If you and the professor can build into the assignment ways for students to "publish" to a wider audience, writing may improve simply because students will be interested in communicating their ideas as clearly as possible to the public.

This chapter discusses ways for your students to publish their work to their classmates or to a larger institutional audience.

Classroom Publishing

Classroom publishing has many of the benefits of more professional publishing but on a much less threatening scale. Students will likely be motivated to write well when they know their work will be read and reviewed by their peers, not just by some distant TA or professor. They also tend to think more concretely in terms of their audience as they write, wondering, for example, "Will Bill and Allison be able to understand what I'm saying?" Because of this audience orientation, students' writing is more likely to be clear and persuasive. Finally, students who know their work will be published to their class are more likely to think of themselves as writers, not just students doing something for a grade. As they see the honest reactions of their classmates to their ideas, they come to understand that the real reason for writing is to share their interpretation of the world with others, and they have the heady experience of seeing their writing influence others.

Classroom publishing can take many forms, and many are very simple to set up. Talk with your professor about ways that might work in your class. The following are some possibilities to start you thinking.

ORAL PRESENTATIONS

In a small class, students could read their papers aloud and respond to questions after the reading. Or you could set up the class like a professional conference, with concurrent sessions, so the students present their work to small subsets of the class.

One university professor has each of his students present a major paper to the class once during the semester. The students must post their papers to the class Web site the week before their scheduled presentations. Everyone in the class reads the papers, and two students are assigned to come prepared with challenging questions about the papers. On the scheduled presentation day, the writers must present their papers and also respond to challenges from the assigned reviewers and other class members. The professor finds that this system makes the students feel much more responsible for the content and quality of their papers.

CLASS BOOKS

Collect single-spaced copies of final papers from the students. Have these copied together to form a class book. Students could pay the copying costs, and the resulting book could become a class text. Have the students read the book and respond to it in some way.

One way to use such a class book is to base one of the questions in the final exam on the papers, either on the content or on the writing style. A question on a history exam might ask, "What are the qualities of a good historiography? Cite examples from the papers included in the class book to illustrate these good qualities."

POSTERS

In many disciplines poster presentations are a common professional way of publishing ideas. Apply this publishing format to your class. Assign students to prepare a poster representing their findings. (You will need to give them guidelines for doing this effectively.) On "poster day" half the class stands by their posters, ready to explain their findings, while the other half wanders about the room learning from their classmates. When half the class period is over, switch roles.

In a large biology class, for example, students are assigned in groups to prepare a poster on a particular issue of current importance, such as the thinning of the ozone layer or the decrease of rain forests. The posters are displayed over a couple of days in the student union. Knowing that their work will be public to the entire university, students take a great deal of care with the posters, completing thorough research and displaying it in a professional format. TAs evaluate the quality of the research by observing the posters, asking the students pertinent questions, and judging the quality of their responses.

Institutional Publishing

Many schools offer opportunities for student work to be published in peer-reviewed settings. Encouraging your students to participate has many advantages.

First, students understand that their writing is important on a larger scale than just within the classroom. Second, they learn about the peer-review process: how to prepare a piece for submission by following specific guidelines, how to learn from rejection (if it happens), and how to work with the organizers or editors for final publication (if they are accepted). Third, having published in these settings will look very impressive when your students apply for jobs or graduate school. Perhaps most important, success in this kind of publishing will give your students encouragement to continue writing and to continue becoming better writers. Be aware of the various publishing opportunities available at your school so that you can share this information with your students. Let your students know the importance of this kind of publication and encourage them to submit their best work.

Teaching Tip: Publication of Students' Work

You can improve your students' chances of winning contests and being accepted for symposia or journals by coaching them in certain skills, including audience awareness, creativity, and following publication guidelines.

- **Audience awareness.** Each contest, symposium, and journal usually has particular criteria. Submitting an essay that did not meet those criteria would be a waste of time, for it would never be selected. Teach students to carefully read and follow the guidelines for submission. Another good idea is for students to read the winning entries or selected submissions from previous years. If these publishing opportunities are local, students could even talk to the organizers to get an idea of what they are looking for. Then they could revise their submissions to fit these expectations more completely.

- **Creativity.** Though submissions must meet the basic criteria for acceptance, to stand out from other submissions students should also demonstrate creativity in responding to those criteria. Encourage your students to enhance the creative element in their papers as they prepare them for submission.

- **Publication guidelines.** Teach students that the detailed instructions for submission exist to simplify the review process. Page limits, style guidelines, and documentation procedures should all be adhered to strictly if students want to improve their chances for winning or being accepted.

CONTESTS

Many departments offer contests for the best papers in a certain area, and sometimes school-wide essay contests are available. Often private donors who want to reward quality student writing award substantial prize money for these contests. Also, academic honor societies, such as Phi Kappa Phi, sponsor writing contests each year for the best freshman, sophomore, junior, and senior papers.

Take the initiative to find what contests may be applicable for your students and encourage them to apply.

SYMPOSIA

Sometimes departments sponsor annual symposia, meetings or conferences to encourage discussion on a topic. These symposia provide students with opportunities to present their papers, after having been carefully reviewed and selected, in a conference-like setting. Participating in symposia gives students a chance to learn how professionals share and defend their findings orally and visually, using overhead slides, charts, or computer-aided presentations.

One university department instituted a reviewed symposium for excellent student papers that had been written that year. Over the next several years, department members found that the quality of students' papers seemed to improve overall as the students saw participation in the symposium as a goal and academic honor.

JOURNALS

Many departments are now publishing their own journals of quality student research. These journals usually mimic professional scholarly journals' review and editing processes and slick, attractive layouts. With faculty guidance, students serve as editors and also are often responsible for the graphic design and other production elements. The review process for these journals can be very competitive, so the publication credit looks impressive on a graduate school application. Once chosen, students have the invaluable experience of working with the editors to prepare final copy for the journal, and they learn firsthand the importance of revising for a particular purpose. Find out if your department sponsors a student journal; if so, be sure to encourage your students to submit their best work for publication consideration.

Technology Tactics

If the technology is available, consider creating and using a class Web site to facilitate classroom publishing and to encourage submission to contests and journals.

- **Online publishing.** Use your class Web site to post your students' papers. Require the class to read and comment on a certain number of them. Discuss the comments in class.
- **Submission information.** You can also post on your Web site a list of appropriate contests and journals to which your students may submit their work. Include pertinent requirements and guidelines. You can also include links to specific contest, symposium, and journal Web sites so that students can explore submission criteria in depth on their own.

Conclusion

Encouraging your students to publish will help them want to be better writers. When you read an outstanding paper, next to the *A* grade take time to write something like, "Why don't you submit this to the XYZ Symposium? I think you have a good chance of being accepted." Showing this kind of confidence in students will encourage them to feel that they can contribute to a larger community. They will also understand that their writing matters.

Chapter Checklist

☐ Provide ways for students to publish their work in the classroom.

☐ Encourage students to submit their writing to institutionally sponsored contests, symposia, or journals.

Applications to Your Own Situation

1. What are some ways your students could publish their work within the classroom?
2. To what contests, symposia, or journals could your students submit their writing? Find out the requirements for submission (including deadlines) and keep this information available to share with students.

Working with Your Professor

1. Discuss with your professor some of your ideas for publishing student writing and whether this would work for your class. If you agree to do some kind of publishing, work on ways to simplify the logistics.
2. Ask your professor if he or she knows of any institutional publishing opportunities for your students. Add any new ideas to the list you may have compiled in response to Application 2.

PART II

Ways to Teach Writing

CHAPTER 8

One-on-One Writing Conferences (Office Hours)

"This is what we can all do to nourish and strengthen one another: listen to one another very hard, ask hard questions, too, send one another away to work again, and laugh in all the right places."

—Nancy Mairs, *Voice Lessons*

In this chapter you will learn

- how to prepare for and conduct effective one-on-one writing conferences.
- how to use questions to encourage students to take responsibility for their own writing.
- how to use activities to involve students in revision.
- how to use constructive praise to teach and reinforce good skills.

As a TA, you will frequently be able to help students individually during your office hours. When students come to you for help, they may ask you to read their draft and tell them what they need to "fix" in order to get a good grade. You must remember you are there to teach, however, not to rewrite the paper for the student. Even if you think you have a great idea for improving the paper, you must take care not to usurp the student's authority. Remember: This is the student's paper, not yours. The only way the student will learn to write well is by making his or her own decisions about how to revise. Besides, the student—who knows best what he or she has to say—is likely to come up with a better plan for the paper than you could.

This chapter discusses how to conduct effective writing conferences by preparing carefully, using questions and activities to encourage independent thought, teaching skills and concepts as needed, and using praise effectively.

Technology Tactics

It is possible to conduct one-on-one writing conferences online.

- **Asynchronous communication.** Email correspondence in which a period of time elapses between each message and reply is an example of

(continued)

Technology Tactics *(continued)*

asynchronous communication. This type of online writing conference has several benefits. First, you and the student must put all your thoughts in writing, and writing about writing further enhances instruction. Second, because there is a delay in communication, you and the student may take time to thoroughly think through questions and comments before replying. And third, there is an electronic record of your "conversation" that you and the student can print out and refer to later.

- **Synchronous communication.** A conversation that you might have in an online chat room is an example of *synchronous communication.* Just like asynchronous communication, you and the student must put all your thoughts in writing, thereby enhancing the writing instruction. The benefit of synchronous communication, however, is that you and the student may hold a finite conversation in real time on a particular date and at a particular time. If your school does not provide access to an online chat space, you can access free online chat services through Yahoo! at <www.chat.yahoo.com> and MSN at <www.chat.msn.com>. (Registration is required.)

Prepare Carefully

Tell students to come to the conference with a completed draft and specific questions to ask. The following are some typical questions students might ask.

- "Does this fit the assignment?"
- "Is the format all right?"
- "What do you think of the overall structure?"
- "Did I include enough specific information?"
- "Can you understand what I'm saying?"

You can prepare for the conference by anticipating such questions and being sure you understand the assignment and the professor's expectations. If possible, get the student's draft early so you can read it before the conference and consider specific areas that may need attention. Also, have a plan in mind for helping the student. (See the Teaching Tip box on p. 74 for a list of open-ended questions to use during conferences. See also the Teaching Tip box on p. 76 for some hands-on activities to use during conferences.)

Set up your meeting space in a way that allows you and the student to work productively. Be sure you have useful resources available, such as the written assignment instructions, sample papers, any texts the students are writing about, a writing handbook, a dictionary, pencils, and scratch paper. Arrange the table (or desk) and chairs so that you and the student can sit side by side. (See Figure 8.1.)

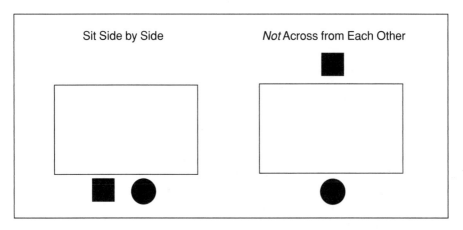

Figure 8.1. Seating Arrangement for a One-on-One Writing Conference

This way, you can both see the paper and you feel like partners. Make sure the student has a pencil in hand, ready to make notes on his or her paper.

Begin the Conference

As the student comes in, greet him or her by name and perhaps just chat for a minute or so. Before long, turn the attention to the concern at hand. Start with a nonthreatening question such as "How's the paper coming along?" or "What can I do to help you?" Try to get the student to lead the conversation.

If you haven't already done so, and if it is shorter than five pages, take the time to read the student's draft before you begin to talk about it. (After all, you can't really advise a student if you haven't read the paper.) Either you or the student can read the paper aloud; there are advantages to either choice. If you read it out loud, the student hears his or her words more objectively. If the student reads it, he or she can stop at will to talk about certain parts that sound "off." Avoid reading the paper silently while the student waits. This could make the student feel awkward or think that you are judging his or her paper.

Use Questions to Draw the Student Out

As you talk together about the paper, guide the student with open-ended questions. (See the Teaching Tip box on p. 74.) Phrase your questions in a way that encourages the student to think. Avoid questions that demand a certain answer. Be truly open to learning from the student.

In the following dialogue, a fictional "TA Terrible" demonstrates an ineffective way of using questions with "Lost Lonnie." (Note: Even if you find yourself on occasion using some of the same tactics TA Terrible does, know that you are *not* a terrible TA. This is tricky stuff, and we all have lapses. You can make up for a bad moment or two with the overall intent and quality of your interaction. You can be TA Terrific.)

TA Terrible: "How can you make this thesis clearer?"

Lost Lonnie: "I don't know. I thought it was clear. I did my best."

Instead, see how TA Terrific draws Lost Lonnie out and helps him discover the problem.

TA Terrific: "Tell me about what you want to say in this paper."

Lost Lonnie: "I want to show how the effects of X and Y cause Z. But . . . I didn't really say that in my paper, did I? I'd better fix that."

Teaching Tip: Questions to Use in One-on-One Conferences

The following questions can be used in one-on-one writing conferences to help students focus their papers, organize their ideas, and discover more specific support.

To Help Writers Focus Their Papers

- "What are you mainly trying to say here?"
- "What do you think the teacher is looking for in the paper?"
- "How does this paper meet the requirements of the assignment?"
- "Why did you choose this topic?"
- "Which is the most important part of the paper? Why?"
- "Is there anything that doesn't seem to fit in the paper?"

To Help Writers Reconsider the Order of Their Ideas

- "What did you tell about first? Second? Third?"
- "Why did you choose this particular order?"
- "What effect would different orders have on the reader?"

To Help Writers Be More Specific

- "Could you explain this to me further?"
- "Tell me more about why you believe this is true. What evidence do you see for this?"
- "Help me to see this in more detail."
- "How might someone disagree with what you are saying?"
- "How could you respond to an alternate interpretation?"
- "Are there any variables you haven't mentioned?"

Questions are usually an excellent way to encourage students to take responsibility for their papers. However, be careful of questions that seem to judge and direct rather than truly invite careful thought. For example, when a TA asks, "Why did you choose this support?" the student might think the TA means, "This support is really bad. I need something different." Instead, a TA could say, "Tell me more about why this is true." This kind of request would still lead to a careful consideration of evidence, without sounding judgmental.

Whether you use questions or requests, be sure to give the student time to think about his or her response. Don't rush in with an answer of your own to "help." Silence is used for thinking; don't let it make you or the student nervous. If the question is particularly difficult, ask the student to write about it while you busy yourself in some other way for a couple minutes, so the student won't be distracted by your looking at him or her. You could go get a drink or look up something in a book.

Practice using questions and requests to encourage student thought, and look forward to hearing the student's answers. Keep a list of general questions handy to refer to during conferences until you get the knack. (See the Teaching Tip box on p. 74.) Your attitude in asking the questions is probably the most important determinant for their effectiveness. You need to be truly interested in what the student thinks. Look forward to learning from the student's answers and enjoy coming to understand the student's ideas.

Use Activities to Get the Student Involved in Revision

Along with questions, activities encourage students to work on their papers during conferences, under your coaching and direction, so you can be sure they know how to apply what you've been talking about. In the following example, TA Terrible simply evaluates Lost Lonnie's paper without giving any guidance on how Lonnie could improve it.

> *TA Terrible:* "Your structure really needs work."
>
> *Lost Lonnie:* "OK . . . I guess I'll fix it . . . later."

On the other hand, TA Terrific uses an activity to get Lonnie working on his paper immediately, under the TA's supervision.

> *TA Terrific:* "Tell me about your structure. How have you organized your paper?"
>
> *Lost Lonnie:* "Gee, I don't know. It just kind of came out that way."
>
> *TA Terrific:* "OK. Let's see what you've got here. Take this pencil and write the main idea for each paragraph in the margin. Then let's see how those ideas connect to each other."

By being guided through an activity that forces him to think about his structure, Lonnie learns a strategy that he can use again on his own in the future. Also, by doing the activity together, the TA can be sure that Lonnie understands the principles she's been trying to teach him.

Teaching Tip: Activities to Use in One-on-One Conferences

The following activities can be used in one-on-one writing conferences to help teach students focus, structure, development, and transition.

To Teach Focus

- Ask students to explain verbally what they are trying to say in print. As the students speak, take notes on their comments. Often students will spontaneously come up with more focused thesis statements.

- Summarize back to students the main things they told you were important to the paper. Suggest that they try to come up with a thesis statement that includes all these aspects.

- Give students some colored highlighters and suggest that they choose one color for each main idea. Then have them go through their paper and highlight in the corresponding color the parts that expand on each idea.

To Teach Structure

- Ask students to write in the margin the main idea for each of their paragraphs.

- Ask students to create a map, chart, or outline of the structure of their paper as it is written. (See pp. 40–42.)

To Teach Development

- Ask students to explain in more detail why they believe a particular claim. Write down the evidence the students mention. Show them your list and ask if some of that information would be good to include in the paragraph.

- Brainstorm with students a list of other points that could be included in a particular section. See how many you can write in just two minutes. Then have students consider if some of the ideas or information should be added to the paper.

To Teach Transition

- Ask students to explain to you the connection between certain parts of the paper. Have them figure out a transition sentence that would make clear that connection. Be sure they write down the sentence.

- Have students underline the paper's major transitions. Ask them to evaluate the effectiveness of their transitions. Are they clear enough? Does the paper need any others?

When Appropriate, Teach Skills and Concepts

Though most often students learn best through careful questioning and guided activities, sometimes they just need instruction. In the following scene, Lost Lonnie has come to his TA for specific assistance.

Lost Lonnie: "I don't understand what a review of the literature is."

TA Terrible: "What do you think it is?"

Lost Lonnie: "I don't know. That's why I came to see you!"

Frustration and anger could follow. Instead, TA Terrific might give a brief definition of a review of the literature and perhaps provide some examples. Then she could ask Lonnie to evaluate how well his review meets that definition. Lonnie would then be ready to apply the definition to his own paper.

But when should you teach indirectly with questions and guided activities, and when should you simply provide the needed information? This decision is a judgment call on your part, but practice and experience will help you make the choice. Consider the following student inquiries:

1. "How should I organize this paper?"
2. "Is this a good thesis?"
3. "What does the professor want?"
4. "What is a lab report?"
5. "Should this paragraph be here?"
6. "Can you understand what I'm saying here?"
7. "What is a thesis?"

Which of these questions should you answer by teaching specific information or concepts? Which of them should you meet with open-ended questions and activities that get the student thinking? The answers would vary depending on the particular student you are teaching and the particular assignment you are working on. However, questions 3, 4, and 7 would probably require specific content and direct teaching. Those questions follow, along with ways to directly teach the information requested and possible follow-up questions to direct the student back to the paper at hand.

Question 3:

"What does the professor want?"

Direct teaching: Read the assignment instructions together, giving added information you might have learned from your meetings with the professor.

Follow-up question: "What ideas do you have for this paper? How do you think you would like to meet these requirements?"

Question 4:

"What is a lab report?"

Direct teaching: Explain exactly what is expected in a lab report. Show examples of good lab reports.

Follow-up question: "How does your report meet these expectations? How do you want to improve your report?"

Question 7:

"What is a thesis?"

Direct teaching: Describe the qualities of a good thesis, including concepts that are important to your professor. Show an example of a good thesis using a topic unrelated to this paper. (*Do not* create a thesis for the student.)

Follow-up question: "Does your thesis meet these expectations? How could you improve it?"

Direct teaching of concepts is very important. However, when students ask you to make writing decisions for them ("How should I organize this paper?"), direct the responsibility back to them with a question of your own ("Tell me about the organization. Why have you chosen the order that you have?") or an activity ("Let's make an outline of the paper as it is written. Then you can decide if you like it this way or if you want to find a better way."). As you continue to practice this skill, you will learn when to teach directly and when to teach indirectly through questions or activities.

Use Constructive Praise to Build Students' Confidence

When working individually with students, you will want to build their confidence by praising their work. Praising specific good points in students' writing teaches them what they should continue doing. Pointing out when you are truly impressed with a certain aspect of their writing—a great title or a strong transition, for example—warms any writer's heart and can motivate hard work on the rest of the piece.

Praise can be counterproductive to learning if it is used inappropriately, however. Insincere praise will only make the student distrust you. If you give general praise, students may think they don't need to improve. Comparing students to their peers usually just leads to bad feelings. Praise that ignores students' ideas gives the impression that the paper's content is unimportant. Following is an example of a poor use of praise.

TA Terrible: "This is a really great paper. It's better than any other paper I read."

Lost Lonnie: "Gee, I thought I needed to work on it more. I guess I should just turn it in the way it is. I mean . . . now I'm sure I'll get an *A*."

On the other hand, praise that is specifically anchored to certain parts of the paper can teach and reinforce a general principle. Students need to know what they are doing right so that they can do those same things again next time. The following is a good example of using praise to teach.

TA Terrific: "I like the way your thesis clearly predicts the structure of your paper. Notice how each main transition in your paper links back to the thesis."

Lost Lonnie: "Thanks! I worked hard on the thesis and structure. And I can see how the transitions help the reader. But I wonder if I have enough support in the second section. Do you think I need to include more specific evidence? And what about the wording of the conclusion? Do you think it works?"

Used appropriately, praise can motivate original thinking in students, and it can build confidence while leaving room for improvement. Effective praise might address the ideas in the paper, focus on effective writing processes, and value originality. The following are some examples of effective uses of praise.

- "Your ideas on XYZ were very creative. You made me think about the topic in new ways."

- "It was easy to follow your argument because the structure of your paper follows the plan you set forth in your introduction."

- "The evidence in this paragraph is compelling. These quotes from the text convince me of your claim."

- "Using the colon in this sentence really sets up the reader for the startling assertion you make."

- "Notice how the sentences in this paragraph connect to each other. You do a good job repeating key words to keep the paragraph unified."

In your conferences use praise liberally, but make sure it is sincere and specific, not just meant to make the student feel good. In other words, make sure your praise is *constructive*.

Conclusion

One-on-one writing conferences are in many ways the ideal teaching situation because you can tailor the teaching activities to the particular needs of an individual student, and you can coach specific skills as the student writes.

For more effective writing conferences, prepare carefully, help the student to feel comfortable as you begin, teach through questions and activities, and use specific, sincere praise to encourage progress. Before completing a conference, ask the student, "What are you going to do with the paper next?" Suggest writing down the main areas to work on so that the student will remember to practice the skills he or she has been learning. Then follow up. Ask about progress next time you see the student. When you grade the final draft, point out areas of improvement. Show that you care about the student's learning.

Chapter Checklist

☐ Encourage students to come to conferences prepared with plans, specific questions, and all the necessary materials (drafts, resources, notes, etc.).

☐ Have the assignment sheet, a writing handbook, a dictionary, and scratch paper available. Be sure you understand the assignment and the professor's priorities.

(continued)

Chapter Checklist *(continued)*

☐ Try to read the draft before you meet with a student. Think of a plan for helping the student address the paper's weaknesses.

☐ Sit side by side, with the writing project where you both can see it.

☐ Use open-ended questions and specific activities to encourage students to evaluate their own writing. Let them have "power of the pen."

☐ Follow up and be supportive. Determine if the students have had problems implementing the plans and changes you discussed.

Applications to Your Own Situation

1. Draft a dialogue for a bad conference in your discipline. Then draft a dialogue for a model good conference.
2. Perform one of these dialogues in front of a group of TAs and discuss it.
3. Think of five open-ended questions you could use when meeting with a student in your class. Keep the list nearby during conferences as a handy reference.
4. What might be a common problem for a student completing a writing assignment in your class? Devise an exercise that would help a student address that problem during a conference.

Working with Your Professor

1. Ask your professor what specific expectations for conferences he or she may have.
2. Discuss the possibility of requiring students to have a conference with you before a paper is due. Ask what the student should bring—such as a thesis statement, an outline, a bibliography, and/or an early draft—to the conference.

CHAPTER 9

In-Class Help Sessions and Workshops

> *"Tell me and I forget. Show me and I remember.*
> *Involve me and I understand."*
>
> —Chinese proverb

In this chapter you will learn

■ how to help groups of students practice and improve their writing skills.

When many students need help with the same kind of problem, you can teach skills more efficiently in a group setting. Maybe you've noticed a certain problem has come up consistently in the last set of papers and you want to avoid seeing the same problem next time. Perhaps you've heard from several students that they are confused about the requirements for the assignment, and you suppose that even more students are confused but are afraid to tell you. Possibly you've noticed that students are having trouble reading scholarly papers as they do their research. A group workshop is an excellent way not only to teach skills to the whole class at once but also to allow students opportunities to practice those skills.

Group teaching could occur in many settings. Perhaps as a TA you already have responsibility for a required out-of-class help session. Perhaps your professor might let you take some time during class. You might offer an optional help session for those who have a certain concern with the assignment. In any case, planning this workshop well is essential to its success, and this chapter will help you do just that.

Planning a Workshop

As you plan, remember that students learn best by doing, especially when they are learning a skill, such as writing. You wouldn't teach children to swim by lecturing in front of a chalkboard. Instead, you jump in the water with them and guide their efforts as they practice. In much the same way, in your writing help session or workshop, you teach a brief mini-lesson, then allow time for students to actually practice while you move among them advising and giving feedback on their progress.

Teaching Tip: The Flexible Lesson Plan

Teachers need to plan their lessons very carefully, but while actually teaching the lessons they need to monitor the reactions of the students and be willing to adapt the plan to meet the needs of the students as they are taught. For example, you may find that the students are not catching on to the concepts as quickly as you expected and decide in the middle of the lesson to cut the last activity so you can have more time to reinforce the first concept. On the other hand, the activities you had planned may move along more smoothly and rapidly than you had expected, and you may find you have some extra time. On the spot you will need to decide what would be the most effective use of that time.

It will be easier to make these spontaneous adaptations if you have a firm idea of the most important concepts you want to teach, work possible modifications into your lesson plan, watch the clock, and, above all, are sensitive to the needs of your students.

- **Know what matters most.** As you prepare the lesson, decide on a teaching objective and understand how each aspect of the lesson works together to reinforce that objective. Having that objective firmly in mind will allow you to adapt the lesson to the particular needs of the moment and still teach the important concepts.

- **Plan possible modifications.** In your written lesson plan, include notes for possible adaptations. You might write, "if time, have a pair share," or "this activity could be optional." If an activity later in the lesson plan is absolutely essential, write in big letters something like this: "SKIP HERE AT 11:30, NO MATTER WHAT."

- **Watch the time.** Have a watch or a clock where you can easily see the time. Be aware of where you are in your plan and how much time you have remaining.

- **Be sensitive to the needs of your students.** Listen and watch your students to recognize what their needs are. Follow their cues. If they have questions that are important to them and to their learning, take the time to answer them, even if this wasn't in your plan. Meeting the needs of the students at the place they are is more important than "covering" everything you had planned.

Be sure that you are realistic about time constraints. Most often activities take longer than you expect. Be flexible—plan more activities than you think you will need, but be prepared to cut out activities if you run out of time. (See the Teaching Tip box.) Also be aware of logistical considerations. How will people move into groups? Will you need to distribute materials? Planning ahead for such contingencies will add to the success of your workshop. The following questions and prompts will help you plan effectively.

- **Identify the needs of the students at this stage. What do they need help with? What common concerns do they have?** To determine the students' needs, think about the writing process. What step of the writing process should they be working on as they progress toward the final document? Also think about questions students have been asking or problems you have observed as you checked their assignments. You might choose to do a workshop on understanding the assignment, finding a topic, doing research, reading and evaluating sources, creating an argumentative thesis, summarizing, paraphrasing, documentation, style, mechanics, or format. Limit the scope of your presentation to a skill or principle that you can teach in the time you have.

- **Plan ways to teach the skill or briefly demonstrate the principles in a very short mini-lesson.** Use about 10 to 20 percent of your time (five to ten minutes of a fifty-minute period; one to two minutes of a ten-minute presentation) to show a need to learn this material and teach the skill. In a workshop on thesis statements, you might explain the qualities of a good thesis statement, then show three or four samples ranging from bad to good. In a workshop on documentation, you could explain why we need to identify the sources of ideas we use in our writing and then show an example of a paragraph that properly cites the sources used.

- **How can the students practice applying the skill, preferably in a way that allows them to work on the paper they are writing?** People learn best when they actively apply what they learned immediately after learning it. Devise an activity in which the students practice the skill you have just taught. This activity portion of the workshop should take about 60 to 70 percent of the time allotted (thirty to thirty-five minutes out of fifty; six to seven minutes out of ten). In the thesis statement workshop, students could work individually on revising their own thesis, and then in groups of three to four respond to each others' theses. In the documentation workshop, you could have students find the correct bibliographic format for sources they will use in their papers.

- **Plan a way to sum up and reinforce what the students have learned and applied.** During the last 10 to 20 percent of the period, do something that reminds the students of the principles and skills they have learned. If time is short, you might simply review the qualities of a good thesis statement or the important parts of a clear citation. If you have a little more time, you might have students share good theses they have written or well-documented paragraphs. You want to be sure that no one leaves the workshop unclear about what they have learned.

- **How much time is available? What materials will you need? What might go wrong?** Assign time limits to each activity. Also list what materials will be needed. Try to plan ahead to avoid problems with logistics or timing. Use a grid, like the one in Table 9.1, to help you organize. After you have planned the workshop carefully, realize that everything will not go as planned. That's part of the fun of teaching! The students will bring their own experiences to your workshop, and you will need to adjust and modify to meet their particular needs. Just be sure that you know clearly what your main goal is; as you make adjustments, see that you still meet that goal.

TABLE 9.1.
A Sample Grid for Planning a Workshop

Time	Activity	Materials Needed
	Opening	
	Mini-lesson	
	Activity	
	(Activity)	
	Closing	

Example 9.1 features a plan for a workshop on understanding an assignment. Notice how answering the questions and filling in the chart force the instructor to think about time for and logistics of the activities. (A blank, downloadable version of this Workshop Planning Sheet is available at <bedford stmartins.com/ta_guide>.)

EXAMPLE 9.1.   A Model Workshop Planning Sheet

WORKSHOP PLANNING SHEET

1. Identify the needs of the students at this stage. What do they need help with? What common concerns do they have?

   The students have trouble understanding the assignment and getting

   started on it.

2. Plan ways to teach the skill or briefly demonstrate the principles in a very short mini-lesson.

   Make a transparency of the assignment instructions to put on the

   overhead projector. Explain the most important qualities the professor is

   looking for.

3. How can the students practice applying the skill, preferably in a way that allows them to work on the paper they are writing?

   Have the students take out the plans they brought with them and consider how to adapt them to meet the needs of the assignment more fully. Then, group the students into threes to discuss the plans together. Provide questions to guide the discussion.

4. Plan a way to sum up and reinforce what the students have learned and applied.

Listen in during the group discussions, and then choose two or three good plans. Ask those students to sketch their plans on a transparency for the class to see. Discuss why these examples are an appropriate response to the assignment, and how the paper might develop from this plan. Briefly explain the next steps in the process (research? drafting? experimental design?).

Time	Activity	Materials Needed
Preparation	Have students come with the plans and research materials they already have.	
5 min	Introduction: Explain that students have seemed confused about the assignment.	
10 min	Mini-lesson: Look at the assignment instructions together. Discuss the main expectations. Demonstrate clustering.	Overhead projector; transparencies of assignment instructions and sample papers; chalk board and chalk
5–10 min	Working from the plans they brought, students individually cluster or outline a plan for their papers. Walk around, look at the plans that are developing, and answer questions as they come up.	

(continued)

EXAMPLE 9.1.   *(continued)*

Time	Activity	Materials Needed
15 min	Students meet in groups of three to share plans and discuss how well these meet the requirements of the assignment. Walk around and listen in on the discussions. Be available to answer questions. Look for plans that seem to meet the needs of the assignment well. During the last five minutes of discussion, have two students write their good plans on a transparency to share with the class.	Keep the transparency of assignment instructions on the overhead projector. Perhaps also provide a handout with some specific questions to guide the group discussions of the plans.
5–10 min	Look at sample plans together. Discuss how these plans meet the needs of the assignment.	
5 min	Closing: Review the main requirements for the assignment. Discuss briefly the next step in the process, and encourage them to get started on that.	

Ideas for Workshop Activities

To have a good workshop, plan activities that involve the students in developing writing skills. To make these activities useful to the students, be sure to start your planning by thinking first of what the students need to learn, then think of how they can learn that skill by doing something in connection to their own paper. If the students need to learn how to use topic sentences in paragraphs, prepare activities that will help them see the importance of topic sentences, and then practice improving the topic sentences in their own papers. The activities need to teach a general skill *and* apply to the writing the students are currently engaged in.

The following is a list of possible activities you could use in workshops to teach certain skills. These ideas are just to start you thinking. More ideas are also available in Chapters 3 through 7, on the writing process. You will be able to think of adaptations, improvements, or entirely new techniques that will be especially applicable for your students.

- **Choosing a limited topic.** Put the main topic for the paper in the center of the chalk board. Have students call out ways to develop the topic, writing a cluster of their ideas as they are called out. After you have the board covered with possibilities, ask what would be an appropriately limited topic for a paper of this scope. Help them see just how specific they can be.

- **Crafting a good thesis statement.** Have students bring their tentative thesis statements to the workshop. Put the statements into a container. After discussing the qualities of a good thesis, draw out the theses at random and ask the class what is good about each thesis statement and what could be improved on. (Get student permission to do this.)

- **Reading a research article.** Explain the main parts of a scientific research article, and then pass out a relatively short example. Assign each small group to analyze a different part of the article: the abstract, introduction, review of literature, results, discussion, or conclusion. Have each group report on the type of information and the style in the section they analyzed. As a class, talk about how the parts work together and consider good strategies for reading such research articles.

- **Finding an appropriate structure.** Divide the class into small groups. Have each group make a map of a professional piece of writing they have previously read. Put the main idea in a box at the top and then, flow-chart fashion, show the movement of ideas in support of the thesis statement. Have them make their charts on large paper or transparency film to share with the class. Later, have students chart the structure of their own papers.

- **Developing paragraph coherence.** Find two model paragraphs, one with good coherence and one without. Cut the sentences apart and have students in groups try to reassemble the paragraphs. The good paragraph should be fairly easy to reassemble, while the poor one will be hard. Later, have students cut one of their own paragraphs into sentences and see if a partner can put it back together in order.

- **Developing ideas.** Take ten minutes for a pair share. For five minutes, one person listens to the other, asking good questions to draw out ideas for the paper. Then have the students switch roles.

- **Identifying and improving transitions.** Bring a model paper (professional or student) with good transitions. Show the paper on the overhead projector and have students identify the transitions. Discuss how the transitions help the reader. Have students look at their own papers to see how they could improve their transitions.

- **Creating good introductions.** Copy good introductory paragraphs from the last set of papers you graded. Take five or ten minutes in class to show these on an overhead projector. Point out what makes these introductions work. (Get student permission to do this.)

- **Incorporating sources correctly.** Prepare a handout with several quotations from different sources on the same topic. Put students in teams to write a paragraph citing those quotations appropriately to prove some claim. Require that each paragraph include a direct quote, a summary, and a paraphrase. (Note: A humorous topic makes these paragraphs more interesting.)

■ **Editing.** From each student's paper, choose one sentence that could be improved by careful editing. Copy the sentences on a handout and have the students in groups decide how to improve the sentences. (Get student permission to do this.)

■ **Practicing self-evaluation.** Obtain sample papers from a previous class, with permission to use them anonymously as teaching aids. In groups, have students evaluate the papers using the scoring guide provided for the paper. Compare the scores given by the various groups and discuss differences. Then have students use the same scoring guide to evaluate their own drafts and make plans for revision.

Technology Tactics

Visual aids help students to focus their attention on the concepts you are teaching, and they also allow you to present models of writing skills. Various forms of technology can be used, from a simple chalk board to a computer presentation. Your visuals will be more effective if you know a few simple techniques for preparing various kinds of visual aids.

■ **Chalk board or white board.** These are perhaps the simplest form of visual aid and many times the most effective. Simply writing an unfamiliar term or an example sentence on the board can clarify your point. When you write on the board, write large enough and clearly enough that everyone can read your message. Another tip: When you erase, move your arm up and down rather than side to side. Then your "tail" won't wag.

■ **Overhead transparencies.** When you use an overhead projector, you are able to face your class while you write or refer to visuals. Another advantage over the chalk board is being able to prepare the transparencies ahead of time in printed form. Transparencies are easier to read if you use a larger font (at least 14 point) and a sans serif font (such as Arial). Don't try to crowd too much information on a single transparency. A simple layout including effective use of white space will be more effective.

■ **Computer presentations.** If you have a lot of information to present in a short period of time, you may want to use a computer presentation program (such as Microsoft PowerPoint) to prepare your lesson. The program will provide templates for your slides and prompt you through the preparation of your presentation. The technology will allow you to easily include illustrations and even video clips. Although many animation options are available, don't be tempted to overdo them. A lot of razzle dazzle can distract from communicating information clearly. Also try not to let the slides become a series of bulleted lists. Finally, and probably most important, bring along transparencies of your slides, just in case the computer/projector system refuses to cooperate. As you consider using this format to present your lesson, realize that this is probably the least flexible format. A computer presentation may limit the amount of classroom interaction you have.

Conclusion

These in-class help sessions or workshops can last five minutes or fifty. The ctivities can be complex or simple. Use whatever time and circumstances you can to teach the students the skills they need to write successfully in your discipline. Once you start thinking in terms of workshops, you will see opportunities to use them, and you will think of activities that will both teach and allow for practice.

Chapter Checklist

☐ Plan in-class help sessions and workshops so that most of the time is used for guided practice of a specific skill in the context of the students' own writing.

☐ Plan carefully to use time well, but be flexible while teaching. Make adjustments to your plan as necessary.

☐ Be creative in planning teaching activities.

Applications to Your Own Situation

1. Look over the class syllabus and assignments. What skills will the students need to learn in order to be successful in writing for the course? Come up with a list of problems that students might have with the course's writing assignments.

2. Choose one of the problems you identified in Application 1. Using the workshop planning sheet in Example 9.1, plan a fifty-minute workshop to teach the necessary skills. Next, condense that plan down to a ten-minute workshop. Keep both plans handy.

3. Think about times and places when you might be able to offer workshops on writing. Could you use five or ten minutes in class? Could you offer an out-of-class help session? Come up with a plan for what would work best for your situation.

Working with Your Professor

1. Discuss with your professor writing skills the students might need to learn as a group. You might refer to common problems on a set of papers or commonly asked questions.

2. Ask your professor where might be the best place to teach these skills. Some possibilities might include an in-class workshop, a voluntary outside-of-class help session (offer extra credit points for coming, perhaps), a required outside-of-class help session (points given for coming), or a regularly scheduled TA-led group meeting.

3. Determine together how much time you should use for the workshop.

4. Share your lesson plans with your professor to get his or her sugges-
    tions. Ask for sample papers or other materials he or she may be able to
    provide.
5. Follow up with your professor by discussing how the workshop went.
    Together, make plans for improving your next workshop.

CHAPTER 10

Commenting on Student Writing

"The writing teacher must not be a judge, but a physician.
His job is not to punish, but to heal."

—Donald M. Murray

In this chapter you will learn

- about problems inherent in communicating with students through written commentary.
- how to write comments that promote improved writing skills.
- how to provide a positive learning environment through your commentary.
- practical guidelines for writing effective commentary.
- time-saving strategies.

One day the students in your class will bring papers to class, and you will head home with a stack of student writing to respond to. When that day comes, you will probably feel overwhelmed with the responsibility of commenting on all those papers. How will you know what to say? How can you write anything helpful in those tiny one-inch margins? How will you know if the students will understand what you say, or if they will even read your comments?

At times like this, it is good to remember that writing comments on student papers is just another writing situation, just like writing a letter, report, or proposal. You will do a better job if you first think about your audience and your purpose, then select the content of your comments with the intent of meeting your audience's needs. This chapter explores the problems inherent in both reading and writing commentary, considers how comments can more clearly meet the needs of your students, and provides specific guidelines and time-saving strategies.

Problems in Communicating through Written Commentary

When students look at the comments scribbled on their papers, their initial reaction may be bewilderment. The following thoughts likely reflect the feelings of many students.

Confused and angry, he stared at the red marks on his paper. He had awked again. And he had fragged. He always awked and fragged. On every theme, a couple of awks and a frag or two. And the inevitable puncs and sp's. . . . How do you keep from awking, he asked himself.[1]

Although this situation is fictional, it is probably not far from the truth. The cryptic and sometimes illegible comments and symbols scribbled in the margins of papers are often misunderstood by the student writer—and sometimes not even read before the grade is noted and the paper is tossed in the trash.

Sometimes students simply do not understand what the teacher is saying, and that misunderstanding can lead to anger and frustration. A 1990 study reported students' reactions to teachers' written comments. When the comment said "Needs to be more concise," students' reactions included "I thought you wanted details and support" and "Define 'concise.'" When told "Be more specific," the students replied, "*You* be more specific," "I tried and it didn't pay off," and "It's going to be too long then." In response to "Try harder!" students explained, "I did try!" and "Baloney! You don't know how hard I tried."[2] Vague, negative comments seemed to annoy students rather than make them want to try harder.

Another study found that some marginal comments actually discouraged students from doing their own revision. Instead of thinking carefully about how to improve the paper, students would simply try to "fix" errors the teacher marked.[3] For example, when most comments focus on punctuation and style with only a general endnote about the need for a better thesis statement, the student will simply try to correct surface errors rather than attempt to solve the more serious problem of focus.

Such confusion is not surprising considering the many difficulties inherent in writing marginal comments: There is no space to fully explain yourself, you have little time to write, and, if you change your mind, it is hard to change your comments. Perhaps this is the reason Nancy Sommers found that most teachers' comments "were not text-specific and could be interchanged, rubber-stamped, from text to text."[4] Faced with an imposing stack of papers and little time for response, it is easy to fall into the "rubber stamp" mode of communication. These "one-size-fits-all" comments, however, often do not mean anything to our students.

Another complicating factor for teachers is a lack of audience focus. Beth Hoger points out that teachers are faced with a complicated and interconnected array of influences. As you read student papers, you are thinking of the individual student, of course, but also of a number of unseen audiences, as illustrated in Table 10.1.[5]

Your task as a TA is even more complicated. You must also think about the professor supervising your work and wonder, "How would he or she respond to this paper? Am I writing what I should? What if the student disagrees with me and complains to the professor?" Trying to meet the needs of all these audiences within the limits of space and time can feel daunting.

The response task is further complicated by the physical circumstances influencing the reading. You can't read all the papers simultaneously, so likely you'll read some papers when you're rested, some when you're tired; some

TABLE 10.1.
A Teacher's Thoughts and Concerns When Grading Students' Papers

Thinking of:	*The teacher wonders:*
The whole class	"Are my responses fair and equitable?"
The department	"Am I preparing the students for future work in the major?"
The institution	"Will I have an appropriate range of grades for this class so I won't be accused of grade inflation?"
The discipline	"How does this student's work and my comments fit into various theoretical orientations?"

when you can concentrate, some when you are distracted. How can you be fair and consistent under such changeable circumstances?

Comments That Promote Improved Writing Skills

Students are therefore likely to be confused or frustrated by our comments, while teachers are constrained by time and space, distracted by competing demands, and likely to be inconsistent because of variable physical circumstances. Given these problems, what can you do to improve your comments? As with every writing problem, a good place to begin is with a consideration of your purpose and the needs of your particular audience—the students who wrote the papers you are reading and who will read the comments you are writing.

Your purpose is to help students improve their writing skills; the students need your guidance to know how to do this. But writing is incredibly complex. Focus, organization, development, paragraphing, sentence structure, word choice, and grammar comprise only a bare outline of the many skills a writer must master. How do you guide students in learning these skills? How do you do so in the context of the paper before you? What are some ways to teach skills in the margins of a paper?

For one thing, you need to remember that you cannot teach all of these skills at once. A student who has just learned how to structure a thesis is probably ready to learn about organizing the paper around that thesis, but he or she may get confused if you try to teach him or her every other writing skill at the same time. The comments you write on student papers need to reflect that understanding. Don't overload students by expecting them to skip directly from novice to expert levels.

You can help your students reach the next step by responding as an audience, guiding substantive thought, encouraging skills improvement, and providing a positive, respectful environment for communication.

RESPONDING AS AN AUDIENCE

Writers have a hard time seeing their own work objectively; they need and appreciate feedback that helps them know how others see their work. As Chris

Anson, director of the Writing and Speaking program at North Carolina State University, says, "Writers improve by being read,"[6] but to do this they must know their readers' reactions to their writing. As a TA, you can provide honest but respectful commentary explaining how the students' writing influences you. Peter Elbow, one of the pioneering scholars in process writing, suggests in *Writing Without Teachers* that the best comments are "movies of the mind,"[7] explanations of how you reacted to the writing as you were reading it. Comments such as the following help a student know how you responded to the paper as an audience.

- "I'm confused. How does this paragraph connect to what is above?"
- "I like your use of verbs here."
- "The specific evidence here makes me want to believe you."
- "Thanks for the clear transition."
- "Wait! What if I don't agree with this assumption?"
- "Is this your thesis? I wasn't sure."

GUIDING SUBSTANTIVE THOUGHT

You want your comments about a piece of writing to lead to more critical thinking about the topic, more awareness of purpose, and more consideration of the best means of achieving that purpose. Students want to be challenged; they want to learn how to become better thinkers and writers. Your comments can help students learn to ask questions that will lead to substantive thinking.

- "What is the main thing you are trying to say here?"
- "How do these parts fit together?"
- "What are some counterarguments to your proposal? How would you respond to those counterarguments?"
- "Can you include more evidence for your assertion?"

ENCOURAGING SKILLS IMPROVEMENT

You also want your comments to teach effective writing skills, within the context of a student's own writing. Students understand that they are taking this class in order to learn something, and they expect to be taught. The following are examples of teaching comments.

- "Try changing this list so every item is the same part of speech: all nouns or all verbs."
- "Does this sentence fit in this paragraph? It seems off track."
- "How does this part relate to your thesis?"
- "Could you make your overall plan clearer in the introduction?"

PROVIDING A POSITIVE ENVIRONMENT

Students are sensitive about their writing. Perhaps because writing requires so much personal involvement, students generally take negative comments about their writing much more personally than a bad score on a math assignment. As a TA, you don't want to discourage students from trying harder. Avoid comments—such as "bad thinking" or "didn't you even read the assignment?"—that may seem to categorically degrade a paper or the student.

Instead, you need to show respect for the writer's ideas. Respond to the ideas presented in the paper, not just the way they are written. This indicates that you value what the student is saying. Also, using questions is a good way to show that you expect the student to be responsible for making the final decisions about revision, that you are not taking their authority away. Responding as an audience takes the sting away ("I'm confused," rather than "you don't make sense"). Here are a few more ideas for comments that show respect for the student while teaching.

- "Good observation!"
- "I've noticed this too. But what do you think about XYZ?"
- "Paragraph 2 is especially well developed. See if you can make paragraph 5 just as convincing."
- "Can you say this more directly? I think you're on the right track here, but I can't follow the sentence."
- "I'm lost. Try a stronger transition to show the connection here."

One easy way to lessen the emotional damage of your comments is simply to avoid red pens because red-ink comments on student papers have developed the connotation of being angry, punitive, and discouraging. Instead, use a pencil or a different color of ink, such as green.

Technology Tactics

Using tools commonly available in most word-processing programs, you can respond to papers electronically. To simplify collecting and returning papers, students could email their papers to you, and then you can comment on those papers electronically and return them by email.

- **Insert comments.** Using this function, you can easily highlight certain parts of the paper and write comments that are not constrained by the size of a one-inch margin. When the student prints out his or her returned paper, your comments will appear in the margins.
- **Track changes.** This function allows you to make changes, which are identified by strikeovers (for deletions) and underscores in different color fonts (for additions), to a draft. If you use this method of commenting on papers electronically, you must resist the urge to make editing or stylistic corrections. If you do, the students can accept and implement your changes with one click of their mouse and will never have to think for a moment why you suggested those changes.

Guidelines for Writing Effective Commentary

When you have a stack of papers to respond to, where do you start? The following are some guidelines that will make your grading sessions more productive.

READ THE PAPER ONCE WITHOUT MARKING IT

Try reading each paper once without a pencil or pen in your hand. Better yet, read the whole set of papers without marking them. Doing this takes self-restraint. You might think you don't have time for it; this quick reading will actually save you time, however, giving you a good idea of what the main problems are with an individual's work and with the class's work as a whole. You can make decisions about what will be most important to comment on this time around. You may notice that a certain writing problem is common to the whole class and decide to teach that concept to the class as a group. You could teach this skill in a brief five-minute lesson in class or in an out-of-class help session (see Chapters 8 and 9). If there is no time for such teaching, you could distribute a handout that would clarify the concern. Knowing that you will teach the skill in detail in (or out of) class, you will not need to write extensive comments on each paper.

COMMENT ON SUBSTANTIVE ISSUES

A busy TA might be tempted to just circle a few mechanical errors, write a brief end comment like "interesting," and assign a grade. Reading these comments, students might think that nothing really needs to be improved except fixing the spelling. Or students might become discouraged and feel that the grade was assigned arbitrarily and there is no way to improve subsequent papers to get a better grade. Students deserve to understand what they are doing right and what they need to improve.

PICK YOUR BATTLES

Remember that too many comments on too many aspects of writing can confuse students. Pick your battles. After your initial reading, choose what the most important areas are for this writer at this time. What is this writer ready to learn? Decide with your professor what your priorities are for this assignment. If the professor has prepared a scoring guide (see Chapter 11), those areas will direct your response. The following is a possible list of areas to consider, in descending order of importance.[8]

1. Does the draft follow the assignment?
2. Is there an appropriate controlling focus?
3. Are the ideas strongly developed?
4. Is there strong overall structure?
5. Are the paragraphs structured carefully and well developed?
6. Is there sufficient specific support to develop the ideas?
7. Are the sentences clear, effective, and error free?
8. Are there patterns of error that should be addressed?

Don't try to deal with these all at once. If the draft does not have a clear focus or a strong structure, that is what you should comment on. If you see clear focus, structure, and paragraphing, then you can direct your attention to development or sentence-level concerns. Respond to a couple of the most important issues in ways that will encourage substantive revision. Robert Connors and Cheryl Glenn, the authors of *The New St. Martin's Guide to Teaching Writing*, suggest only three or four marginal comments on each page.[9]

RESPOND RESPECTFULLY AS A READER

Discuss the content of the piece as though you were talking with a peer. Ask important questions. Point out places where you were moved or convinced. Point out places where you were confused or disappointed. Use open-ended questions to encourage thinking, and use sincere and well-founded praise to teach what works well.

MAKE IT CLEAR THAT SURFACE ERRORS MATTER, BUT DON'T EDIT THE PAPER

If you "fix" every error, students will not learn to make corrections themselves. Responding to papers can be baffling sometimes; it can be comforting to swoop in and fix something that is clearly wrong—a misspelled word or a comma splice. Resist the urge. Such markings communicate that all you really care about is correct spelling and punctuation. Instead, try marking each error with a check mark in the margin. Or you can carefully edit one paragraph, showing the level of correctness you expect for the whole paper, and leave the rest of the editing to the student. Let the students know they are responsible for correcting all errors. (Offer to help if they really need it.) If there are too many errors, refuse to accept the work until it has been cleaned up.

WRITE A SUBSTANTIVE ENDNOTE TO SUMMARIZE YOUR COMMENTS

As with all comments, the summarizing endnote should be respectful and specific. I like following a three-part structure.

1. Comment specifically on the strengths of the paper.
2. Assess a major problem to work on in the revision or in the next paper.
3. Give specific procedural recommendations for how to go about the revision. You might suggest a thirty-minute freewriting exercise to develop a clearer idea of the specific purpose or going through the paper to determine the main idea of each paragraph before revising the structure. (See Chapter 8 for more ideas on revision strategies.)

Connors and Glenn suggest that the endnote should evaluate the paper's thesis, content, organization, and style as well as recognize the progress the student has made since the last assignment. The endnote should be about 100–150 words long.[10] The following are a writing prompt from a sociology class, a sample student response, and sample teacher's comments.

Is gender identity inherent or learned? Write a brief but well-developed essay that discusses your perspectives on this issue. The essay should be thesis driven and well organized, and it should draw upon your personal experiences to support its argument.

Good
example! I
like the
detail

When my sister-in-law had a baby boy, she told me that she was going to raise him without gender bias. She gave him toys that were pink and toys that were (blue.) She was sure that this would allow him to grow up in an (organic) manner, without having to conform to society's ideas of masculinity or femininity. But she soon found that when she offered him the choice between a doll and a truck, he'd throw down the doll and race for the truck. He made airplane noises, he started shooting fake guns around the house (even though she didn't allow him to watch violent TV or movies), and he'd yell, wrestle and growl.

What do
you
mean by
organic?

Is this
your the-
sis? What
do you
mean by
"define hu-
mans as
humans?"
Does this
answer
the ques-
tion about
gender
identity?

Even though we as a society often want to define (humans as humans,) there are inherent differences in men and women. My brothers say women simply cannot dunk basketballs, which is why mens professional basketball is more entertaining than (women will ever be.) The different chemical levels in men and women effects desires and moods.

Using
topic sen-
tences
would
help your
reader
see the
focus for
each
paragraph

Women at work always complain about how men can't multitask. They also rail about how men never want to talk or go to the movies women like. On the other hand, they do say men have a greater natural ability to focus. This is why men and women compliment each other.

Even though it's good that we assume equality for all humans, it is important to note that men and women are *different*. Just as we value minority cultural or ethnic groups for their differences while maintaining their equality, we should value men and women's differences and grant them equal rights. The time has come for us to acknowledge that everyone deserves an equal say in this (society.)

Your
paper
doesn't
prepare
us for
this con-
clusion.
What
about
gender
identity?

I like your opening story. It prepares us for a discussion of gender identity, as the professor has requested, and it is detailed and convincing.

The rest of the paper seems to drift to other concerns: gender differences and equal rights. I suggest you rewrite much of this paper. Just answer the question in the thesis and then share specific support for your answer from your own experience. Give us enough detail that we understand why your experience leads you to that conclusion. Before you write, brainstorm to think of other experiences that would support your thesis as effectively as your opening story.

Though you will be rewriting much of this paper, I have circled some word choice problems and underlined some problems with mechanics, just so you will know the kinds of problems to avoid as you rewrite. Use a handbook and dictionary if you have questions, or come see me. I'd be glad to talk to you about any aspect of your revisions.

Teaching Tip: Time-Saving Strategies

Writing comments on student papers is challenging, but it needn't take forever. Often, less is more. A few well-chosen comments focused on a specific need can be more effective than covering a paper with hard-to-understand and perhaps conflicting advice. Remember, you are not to edit or rewrite the paper. You are to encourage revision and improve skills, one step at a time. A few good questions can do that. The following are a few strategies to save you time.

- If a paper is really in trouble, don't even try to help the writer in those inadequate one-inch margins. Simply invite the student to come to your office hours, so you can discuss the revision in more depth and teach the skills the student needs. (See Chapter 8.)

- If a problem is common to many papers in the class, don't take time to explain that problem on every paper. Teach the skill to the class as a whole. (See Chapter 9.)

- Remember that not all kinds of assignments need the same kinds of comments. Some short Writing-to-Learn assignments need only an "OK" or perhaps a brief comment or question. A more extensive paper would require more extensive comments. If the student is likely to revise the paper you are reading, your comments are *formative:* Your purpose is to help the student with that revision, and your comments and suggestions should be substantial. If the paper will not be revised, your comments are *summative:* Your purpose is to explain the grade, and your comments and suggestions can be brief.

- Decide on a reasonable amount of time to spend on each paper, and adhere to that limit. Use a timer if necessary.

Conclusion

Commenting on student papers will always be challenging. Remembering your audience and purpose will help you to write more effectively in the margins of students' papers. Your comments will be most useful when you remember that you are engaging in a conversation with the student. The writing prompt initiated the conversation, the student's paper responds to the prompt, your comments respond to the student, and the student will respond to your comments in the revised draft. Conversations about interesting ideas are almost always satisfying. Look at this conversation in that way, and enjoy the chat.

Chapter Checklist

☐ Remember your overall purpose and your audience as you write commentary.

☐ Follow an effective process for writing comments: Read the papers through first, follow a priority list in deciding what to comment on, and respond respectfully. Make it clear that surface errors matter, but don't edit the paper. Write a substantive endnote to encourage revision of this draft or improvement on the next paper.

☐ Make comments that are both encouraging and challenging. Avoid using red pen for your comments.

☐ Work efficiently. A few well-chosen comments and questions are better than a page covered in difficult-to-decipher comments. Limit the amount of time you spend on each paper.

Applications to Your Own Situation

1. Find a paper you wrote that has your professor's commentary on it. What comments helped you want to revise? What comments helped you learn how to do better next time you wrote a similar paper? What were your reactions to the comments when you first read them? What do you think of them now?

2. Find a student paper that was written for the course you are TAing. Decide what would be the most important issues to address in responding to that paper. Write marginal commentary and an endnote. Share your response with your professor and/or other TAs for the course. Discuss differences in approach. Think of ways to revise your response to be even more effective.

Working with Your Professor

1. When students submit a set of papers, ask your professor to look over some of them with you. Choose two or three at random, and read them together. Ask your professor such questions as the following:
   - "What do you think is the most important problem here?"
   - "What do you think is done well?"

- "Where would you comment on the paper? What would you say?"
- "What would you encourage the student to do next time or in a revision?"

2. Show your professor the set of papers you have responded to. Ask where he or she might agree or disagree with your comments. Ask about problem papers that you didn't know what to do with.

3. With your professor, identify common problems the students are having with their writing. Together devise a plan for teaching the skills the students need or for making the necessary clarifications in the assignment.

CHAPTER 11

Fair and Consistent Evaluation

"Honest criticism is hard to take—especially when it comes from a relative,
a friend, an acquaintance, or a stranger."

—Franklin P. Jones

In this chapter you will learn

- how to develop and use analytic grading rubrics.
- how to develop and use holistic grading rubrics.
- how to assure consistency when more than one grader is working with a class.

Grading papers is probably what you dread most about being a TA. If it is any comfort to you, it is also probably what teachers dread most, and students (as you no doubt know) certainly dread being graded. Evaluating writing seems so subjective, not like correcting a math problem, which is either right or wrong, or an objective test, which has a clear percentage score.

This chapter discusses ways to grade writing both fairly and consistently. To be fair, you must consider the same criteria for each paper and not have more stringent expectations for one student than for another. To be consistent, you want to be sure that you grade the first paper you read according to the same expectations as the last and that one grader uses the same criteria as another for the same assignment.

A good way to assure that grades are both fair and consistent is to have a clearly delineated list of criteria on which to base a grade. Such a list of grading criteria is sometimes called a *grading rubric, grading sheet*, or *scoring guide*. It really doesn't matter what you choose to call it. Preparing such a guide at the time the assignment is made, distributing it to the students to refer to as they write, and using it carefully as you grade will bring about better writing and better grading. Learning how to create and use a grading rubric will lead to more fairness and consistency.

Analytic Grading

Evaluating papers is similar to many other judgments you must make every day. Should you wear a sweater or a coat today? What kind of car should you buy?

Should you tell Sue what you really think of her new pants? When you make judgments like these, you use, either consciously or subconsciously, standards to guide your decision: temperature and weather, price and dependability, Sue's personality and the social consequences of those pants. Determining the relevant criteria makes a reasonable judgment easier to come to. With rational criteria as a guide, you are less likely to be distracted by emotional, irrelevant factors.

Likewise, assigning a grade can become less mystical for you and your students if you develop a list of criteria to guide your grading. Analytic grading relies on an analysis of the various criteria for a good paper in order to assign value. Although you can't reduce an assessment of writing to a purely objective numerical formula, you can break down the main standards you are looking for. If you share these criteria with the students before they write their papers, they will strive to meet those standards and submit a more carefully written paper. Having the criteria will help you to be more consistent in your grading. Whether the paper is read first or last, whether you are feeling cranky or mellow, you will still need to evaluate each of the stated criteria for each paper, which will help your assessment to be more complete and fair. Your professor will probably take most of the responsibility for determining grading criteria; however, this section will help you to better understand what is behind the grading rubric you will use.

DEVELOPING GRADING CRITERIA

To determine what criteria are important in evaluating a paper, consider the purpose of the assignment. If the main purpose of the assignment is to show an ability to synthesize information from a variety of sources, then ability to synthesize should be one of the grading criteria. If the assignment is designed to show that the student is able to describe experimental data clearly, then that goal needs to be included in the criteria.

Grading criteria are most effective if they are customized to each assignment or kind of assignment. Though it may seem easier to use one standard grading rubric for all papers, it is better to have one set of criteria for the lab notebook and another for the research paper, because there are different expectations and purposes for each. The following steps can help you and your professor to develop your own assignment-specific grading rubrics.

List Important Criteria. List all the important qualities of a good paper written in response to that particular assignment. The list for a lab report, for example, might include the following.[1]

- professional presentation, including a letter of transmittal, cover page, abstract or summary, table of contents, list of illustrations, and glossary of terms
- a clear introduction stating the problem or purpose of the experiments, why it is important, and the hypothesis the experiment is to prove
- a literature review that summarizes work that has been published on this problem
- a methods section explaining how the data was gathered

- an interpretation of data/conclusions section that explains the significance of the findings
- visual aids such as drawings, photographs, charts, or graphs
- a conclusion expressing specific recommendations for further research
- a list of sources
- style and mechanics that are clear, effective, and correct

The list for your particular assignment will vary. The following is a list a teacher developed to guide her evaluation of history papers.[2]

- An interesting title and opening paragraph prepare the reader for the paper.
- Issues and events are placed in time and set in a historical context.
- Historical evidence or quotes support claims made by the author.
- Competing historical points of view are considered.
- Structure is coherent and focused, with a summary in the concluding paragraph.
- Presentation, style, and mechanics enhance, rather than detract from, the paper.

With the important elements isolated, you can then add descriptions of what you require in each area. Think of your students as you describe the various requirements. Sometimes a series of questions helps to clarify what you are looking for. If you have a textbook that discusses these elements in more detail, you can refer the students to specific page numbers in the book for further information. A well-prepared grading rubric can serve as a powerful teaching tool. Explain the criteria clearly so students will understand what they need to do to improve.

Decide the Criteria Weighting and Format. Once the important elements of the paper have been determined, work with your professor to decide which elements of these criteria are most important. You may decide that all the criteria are equally important, or you may decide to weight some more heavily than others. There is no one right way. Some teachers like to assign a certain number of points to each criterion, while others explain that each criterion is worth a certain percentage of the final grade. You and the professor will need to decide what best fits the class and requirements of the assignment.

A variety of formats can work for grading rubrics. Will the sum of points, the average of the points, or your feedback determine the grade? You and your professor will need to decide what will work best for you. Examples 11.1 through 11.4 show various grading rubric formats that are used in a variety of courses.

Technology Tactics

Downloadable versions of the grading rubrics in Examples 11.1 through 11.5, as well as other useful forms and worksheets, are available at <bedford stmartins.com/ta_guide>.

EXAMPLE 11.1. Graduated Responses[i]

FSN 445—PAPER GRADING SHEET

Name: _____

1 Content: (25 pts) Is the paper informative, with a clear purpose? Is the Introduction helpful? Do the ideas/concepts develop logically and clearly? Does the conclusion sum up the paper adequately?

Definitely	Mostly	Marginally	Not Really

2 Tone: (4 pts) Are the level of the writing and the use of language appropriate and professional?

Definitely	Mostly	Marginally	Not Really

3 Use of Resources: (4 pts) Was the depth of research adequate? Were reliable sources used? Were ideas paraphrased or summarized honestly and effectively?

Definitely	Mostly	Marginally	Not Really

4 Format: (4 pts) Does the paper follow the required format? Do headings guide the reader through the paper?

Definitely	Mostly	Marginally	Not Really

5 Documentation: (4 pts) Are citations in the text and the reference page correct according to appropriate style?

Definitely	Mostly	Marginally	Not Really

6 Mechanics: (4 pts) Is the paper free from spelling, punctuation, and grammatical errors? Has it been carefully proofread?

Definitely	Mostly	Marginally	Not Really

7 Overall Quality: (5 pts) Is the topic worth writing about? Does the paper hold together well, present sound argument or description, reflect clear thinking? Is it enjoyable to read?

Definitely	Mostly	Marginally	Not Really

Score: _____

---

[i]Thanks to Nora Nyland, Department of Nutrition, Dietetics and Food Services, Brigham Young University (BYU).

EXAMPLE 11.2.   Numerical Responses[ii]

111 GEOL—TERM PAPER BIBLIOGRAPHY EVALUATION SHEET

Name: _____

Grading Criteria

The bibliography will be graded on the quality and number of references (10 is adequate; after 15 I won't look at them), the quality of the annotation, the variety of source types (there must be at least one from each of the categories listed on the assignment sheet), and format (including reference style and order of citation), as well as neatness, grammar, and spelling. Consult the grading sheet below.

Categories	Possible	Earned	Comments
Neatness	10	_____	
Grammar	10	_____	
Spelling and capitalization	10	_____	
Quality of references and category	10	_____	
Clarity and style of annotation	10	_____	
Quality of references	10	_____	
Content and accuracy of summaries	30	_____	
Reference format	10	_____	
Score:	**100**	_____	

[ii]Thanks to Eric Christiansen, Department of Geology, BYU.

EXAMPLE 11.3. Scales[iii]

MFHD 340—GENERAL GRADING CRITERIA FOR SEMESTER PAPERS

Name: _____

Accuracy in using concepts

1 ------- 2 ------- 3 ------- 4 ------- 5 ------- 6 ------- 7 ------- 8 ------- 9 ------- 10

unclear   *very clear concepts,*
definitions   *defined and understood*

Ideas (creativity and quality of thought)

1 ------- 2 ------- 3 ------- 4 ------- 5 ------- 6 ------- 7 ------- 8 ------- 9 ------- 10

shallow,   *substantive,*
mundane   *imaginative*

Support (detail, sufficiency, substantiality, relevance)

1 ------- 2 ------- 3 ------- 4 ------- 5 ------- 6 ------- 7 ------- 8 ------- 9 ------- 10

week, feeble,   *very strong*
fallacious arguments

Organization (unity, coherence, progression)

1 ------- 2 ------- 3 ------- 4 ------- 5 ------- 6 ------- 7 ------- 8 ------- 9 ------- 10

very loose   *very tight*

Technical control (use of spelling, capitalization, punctuation, grammar, APA style)

1 ------- 2 ------- 3 ------- 4 ------- 5 ------- 6 ------- 7 ------- 8 ------- 9 ------- 10

ineffective   *very effective*

Score: _____

[iii]Thanks to David Nelson, Department of Marriage, Family, and Human Development, BYU.

EXAMPLE 11.4. Written Comments[iv]

FIRST YEAR WRITING: HONORS 200 RUBRIC FOR CRITICAL ANALYSIS	
Name: _____	
Organization and Arguments	**Comments**
Thesis clearly communicates topic, focus, and purpose	
Thesis (intro) delineates organization	
Essay covers all aspects promised by thesis	
Logically organized	
Thesis supported by main ideas	
All material is directly on topic	
Main ideas directly related to thesis	
Adequate evidence supports all claims	
Evidence is thoroughly analyzed and explained	
Body paragraphs are well developed, have main ideas, and provide reasons, facts, and examples	
Introduction—attention/introduces topic/leads into thesis	
Conclusion—completion/slightly new idea/not merely a summary	
Analysis, not summary	
Subject Matter	**Comments**
Suitable topic	
Covered completely	
Sound reasoning/no logical fallacies	
Style and Mechanics	**Comments**
Transitions	
Citing textual evidence accurately	
Citing outside evidence accurately	

[iv]Thanks to Kylie Turley, Department of English, BYU.

Concise	
Sentence structure—variety and emphasis	
Grammar	
Punctuation	
Formality	
Passive voice	
Sexist language, slang, clichés, etc.	
Grade: _____ **Drafts:** _____	

USING THE GRADING RUBRIC

Using an analytic grading rubric requires evaluating each aspect of the paper separately. After reading through the paper as a whole, turn to the grading rubric. Determine how successful the paper is in each area. How well focused is the thesis? How well developed are the main points? Are the sentences clear? In each area, show students how successful they were by filling in the points or by marking the graduated continuum. When you want to give students more feedback, write brief notes on the grading guide to explain your evaluation. One of the main advantages of the analytic grading rubric is that it allows you to give students specific feedback on the most important skills you are trying to teach. Students can look at the grading rubric and quickly identify areas that are working and areas that still need work. The analytic guidelines remind you to consider all aspects of the paper when you are assigning the grade and also help you to be both fair and consistent in your grading.

Holistic Grading

Analytic evaluation is good for formative evaluation, because it provides clear expectations for students and guides revision and improvement on future assignments. It can also help with summative evaluation, providing a clear explanation of how the grade was determined. Sometimes such a detailed breakdown of a final grade can be misleading, however. If you have assigned 10 points out of 100 for the presentation of the paper, do you really take only 10 points off if the mechanics and style are so bad that you can barely decipher the meaning? In reality, each aspect of a piece of writing influences all the others, and it is almost impossible to isolate one from another.

Holistic grading is a more unified approach to evaluation. Edward White, a leading authority on writing assessment, points out that holistic grading "allows us to consider writing as more than just the sum of its parts."[3] The holistic grading rubric, rather than breaking down the various elements of a paper, describes the qualities of a paper at various levels of expertise. The guide would describe the qualities of an *A* paper, then a *B* paper, and so forth. To use such a guide, the grader would read the paper and compare it with the descriptions to see which level the paper most closely matches.

To develop a holistic grading rubric, think of the qualities you would expect to find in an *A* paper, *B* paper, *C* paper, and so forth. Write a description of those qualities for each grade designation. Include various important criteria in each description. (See Example 11.5.) Each description should include some discussion of the level of focus, structure, support, paragraphing, style, mechanics, and other criteria you may choose to focus on.

Holistic evaluation works well for giving an overall judgment of a piece of writing. It is especially good for summative evaluation. Though less detailed feedback is included on the grading sheet, the overall assessment is probably very reliable. Holistic evaluation is often used for scoring a large number of essays because it can be done very quickly and with good reliability. It is not as effective for encouraging revision, however, because of the less specific nature of the feedback given.

Teaching Tip: Emotions Vs. Responsibilities

Remember the following points when you are grading your students' writing.

- You may feel terrible about giving a low grade, but you must remember that *not all students are good students.* They may be very much aware of the problems in their papers and have simply chosen not to fix them. They may be expecting the very grade their paper earns.

- You do not "give" grades—students earn them. They make their own choices. You just describe the relative quality of their work using the symbol of a grade.

- Try not to fall into what Connors and Glenn call the "*B* fallacy."[4] Even though you know a paper is only adequate, you may be tempted to still give it a *B* grade. You may think students will be happier and less likely to complain, but you need to remember a *C* grade means average. Assign *B*s only to those papers that are truly above average, and *A*s to the few papers that are in fact exceptional.

- Letter grades have psychological weight. You may find it easier to grade fairly if you use point values or other symbols to show relative merit.

Grade Norming

Whether the assessment is analytic or holistic, it is imperative that students feel their work will be evaluated fairly no matter who is their grader. Students need to feel that the TA will assess their papers in much the same way as the professor. In large classes where more than one grader is evaluating papers, graders

EXAMPLE 11.5.   Holistic Grading Rubric[v]

<table>
<tr><td colspan="2" align="center">**TMA 300—CRITICAL ANALYSIS GRADING RUBRIC**</td></tr>
<tr><td>*A*</td><td>An analysis earning an *A* will have selected a complicated text that requires careful investigation. This investigation will clearly follow a thesis statement that is concrete, unique, and contestable. The analysis will employ at least one critical theory we have studied this semester and will show a familiarity with the purpose, vocabulary, and application of the theory. The paper will have few or no grammatical or mechanical errors. It will be written in a clear, flowing style, with precise word choice and a variety of sentence length. It will have at least three solid critical sources to support or contest its argument. Most important, it will demonstrate deep critical thinking about the text, the theory, and how this impacts some attitude or aspect of society.</td></tr>
<tr><td>*B*</td><td>An analysis earning a *B* will include all of the above, but the writer's discussion of the text and the theory will be less carefully developed. *B* papers may have less than the required bibliographic sources. It will include a high number of stylistic, mechanical, and formatting errors.</td></tr>
<tr><td>*C*</td><td>An analysis earning a *C* will include all of the above, but it will show less evidence of careful thought, will misapply a theory, or be missing any critical bibliographic sources. It will show a greater number of stylistic, mechanical, and formatting errors.</td></tr>
<tr><td>*D*</td><td>An analysis earning a *D* will have more than one error of *C*-level work (for example, less evidence of careful thought *and* misapplication of theory), in addition to having the other characteristics of no higher than *C*-level work. A paper with a substantial number of stylistic, mechanical, and formatting errors and little evidence of careful thought will also earn a *D*.</td></tr>
<tr><td>*F*</td><td>An analysis earning an *F* will have the characteristics of *D*-level work but will also lack either a critical theory or a text.</td></tr>
</table>

need to strive for consistency. Otherwise, students will talk about who got the hard grader and who got the easy grader. They will feel that they got a low grade unfairly, and they will complain to the teacher. Such disparities in assessment lessen the credibility of TAs.

Having "published" grading criteria will help to minimize these problems, but holding regular grade-norming sessions will help even more. In a grade-norming session the professor and all TAs for the course practice grading sample papers together, applying the grading criteria, and explaining the grading decisions they make. Through this practice, the group of graders learns to evaluate

---

[v]Thanks to Megan Sanborn Jones, Department of Theatre and Media Arts, BYU.

papers similarly. Your professor will probably want to take charge in such a session. The following guidelines can serve as a resource for planning and participating.

1. Your professor will select several sample student essays that respond to the same prompt as the group of papers that will be evaluated. Essays representing a range of quality will be represented, from very good to very poor, with several in the medium range. About four to five sample essays is a good number. There should be enough copies for all the participants.

2. Before you begin looking at the sample papers with the group of graders, your professor will review the predetermined grading criteria and clarify any questions you TAs may have. Your professor may choose to use a six-point scale (6 is high, 1 is low) to sidestep the psychological baggage of letter grades. On the other hand, your professor may choose to use the same grading system you will use for the students, so that you become familiar with using it.

3. All of the TAs (graders) will read the essays, and individually assign scores to them, referring to the grading criteria.

4. The graders share their grades for each essay, while your professor writes the range on the chalk board or an overhead transparency. Note the range in grades. If the grades vary by more than one point, your professor will have the high and low graders defend their scores, referring to the grading criteria. Then the graders will reevaluate the contested essay and see if the grades are more in line.

5. Keep doing this until the group is grading the essays relatively consistently.

6. Your professor will have you repeat this exercise as necessary, for new assignments or midway through the semester.

If your professor does not feel that such a large-scale training session is practical in your situation, you could have a more informal discussion with your professor when the papers to be graded are first turned in. Before you start grading, ask your professor to look at one or two papers with you. He or she could explain what to look for in the papers as you read them together, explaining how to apply the grading rubric.

Another good idea is to meet with your professor and/or other TAs after grading the papers and before passing them back. Each grader should bring copies of a paper that was particularly difficult to evaluate. Read the papers together and discuss the best way to respond to and evaluate them. Doing this regularly will help you to feel more confident about the grades you assign.

Conclusion

Evaluating papers will always be a challenging yet necessary task. Students need to know how their writing measures up and what they need to change to become better writers. You are not being fair to your students if you do not grade their writing at regular intervals during the semester to let them know how they are progressing.

Identifying and weighting criteria, using either an analytic or holistic grading rubric, and holding grade-norming sessions can increase your reliability as a grader. Remember that you are not punishing students with a grade; you are simply describing the quality of their work so that they can learn how to write better.

Chapter Checklist

☐ Work with your professor to identify and weight grading criteria.

☐ Help your professor to prepare a clear grading rubric (either analytic or holistic) and make it available to both students and graders.

☐ Participate in grade-norming exercises with other graders so that you are all using the grading rubric consistently.

Applications to Your Own Situation

1. Using a writing assignment for your class, make a list describing important elements that would be found in an excellent paper. Decide how to weight those elements. Prepare an analytic grading rubric for that paper.

2. Using the same criteria as for Application 1, develop a holistic grading rubric. Notice the differences between the two kinds of guides.

Working with Your Professor

1. Discuss grading criteria with your professor and help him or her to refine the criteria.

2. Ask your professor how he or she wants to deal with possible grade complaints. (See Chapter 13 for more on handling student complaints about grades.)

3. If many different TAs grade papers for your class, discuss with your professor the possibility for setting up a grade-norming session to help standardize grading in the class.

4. Ask your professor if he or she would like to hold post-grading sessions where graders share difficult-to-grade papers and discuss ways to respond to them.

CHAPTER 12

Essay Exams, Research Papers, and Collaborative Writing Projects

"Every time a student sits down to write for us, he has to invent the university for the occasion."

—David Bartholomae, "Inventing the University"

In this chapter you will learn

- strategies for developing, assigning, and evaluating essay exams, research papers, and collaborative writing projects.

Position papers, lab notebooks, film analyses, abstracts, reviews of the literature, and case studies all have distinct requirements. Each discipline's writing has its own particular conventions, too many to detail in a book of this sort. You and your professor should work together to determine how to teach students concerning these discipline-specific genres, including information about audience, purpose, context, and conventions of format. A specialized guide to writing in your discipline, such as the ones listed in the Bibliography, will be helpful in understanding expectations for specialized kinds of writing. However, certain forms of writing, such as essay exams, research papers, and collaborative writing projects, are fairly common in many disciplines.

Essay Exams

Exam questions requiring essay responses can assess not only students' command of course material but also their ability to synthesize, analyze, and apply that material in a time-limited situation. To be most effective, the essay questions must be carefully composed, and the responses must be carefully graded.

COMPOSING ESSAY EXAM QUESTIONS

Conventional teaching wisdom says multiple-choice tests are hard to write and easy to grade, while essay tests are easy to write and hard to grade. The truth of the matter is that both kinds of tests are challenging to produce. As a TA, you may not be responsible for composing essay questions on your own, but your professor may ask you for feedback or help with composing an essay exam. This section will give you an understanding of how to compose an essay exam as well as how to grade one.

First, consider whether an essay question is the best way to measure knowledge. Basic factual knowledge is best assessed with an objective question.[1] An essay question is best used when you want students to demonstrate synthesis, analysis, or application of what they have learned. Also think carefully about the scope of the question, which should prompt a response that can be appropriately addressed in the time and space available.[2] If the question is too broad, you will not be able to judge the depth of the students' understanding. If the question is too narrow, students may not be able to demonstrate their overall command of the subject material. Be sure the scope of the question allows the students to meet the purposes of your examination.

Essay questions must be phrased very carefully. If you want to assess synthesis, analysis, or application, design the question so that students are required to do this sort of complex thinking. Define the task you want the students to complete and design the question to match that task.[3] As Edward White points out, such clarity "free[s] students from the enervating, distracting, and often futile labor of guessing what we want, why we want it, and how we will respond."[4]

Use "code" words carefully. Words such as *describe, discuss, compare, contrast, explain,* or *comment* cause problems when students do not understand these words the same way the professor does. A student might think *compare* means to discuss only similarities, whereas the professor wants a response that considers both similarities *and* differences. Or a student might think *discuss* means "write everything you know on this subject," whereas the professor really wants a more specific treatment of the idea. Choose language carefully so that there is no way to misinterpret the directions.[5]

You can help students respond with a unified, carefully considered essay by phrasing questions so that a clear thesis would be formed in response to it. Questions where students must either defend or refute a statement may work best.[6] Also, keep each question short and avoid sub-questions or hints. Although teachers may think they are helping students by adding sub-questions, such a practice may actually lead to poorly thought-out responses, as students just answer the sub-questions in the order given without thinking of the overall plan of their own essay.[7] Similarly, don't dictate the exact structure and content of the response. Students need to be able to compose their own response if they are to demonstrate their understanding of the topic well.[8]

The format of the exam can aid students to do their best. For example, sometimes teachers will provide a number of questions for students to choose from, thinking this will allow students to showcase the information they have learned best. Actually, too many choices can confuse students who might waste their time as they try to decide which question to respond to. Also, all questions are not likely to be of equal difficulty, and students choosing the harder question will be penalized.[9] It is better to give students one well-written question rather than offer a choice of several. (See Table 12.1.) Students will perform better if you specify the point value of the item, approximately how long the response should take, and the grading criteria you will use.[10] This information will help students budget their time and include important information.

TABLE 12.1.
Sample Essay Exam Questions

Less Effective Question	*More Effective Question*
Briefly describe, in detail, the mechanism of reverse transcription.	Explain how a virus inserts its genome into the cell using the reverse transcription of mRNA as an example.
Discuss the current state of the economy.	Is the U.S. economy currently in a recession? Include specific evidence to support your response.
Explain lean manufacturing.	Would implementing lean manufacturing benefit or harm productivity in company X?
How do reality and fantasy interact in *Don Quixote?*	What does Don Quixote's adventure with the windmills suggest about the Golden Age of Spain and the tension between reality and fantasy?
Explain the difference between the continuous model of matter and the molecular model.	When you consider a substance like glass or modeling clay in terms of the continuous model of matter, they seem to be solids, but in terms of the molecular model, they appear to be liquids. Explain why.
Discuss the rational choice paradigm.	What are the pros and cons of using a rational choice paradigm?

GRADING ESSAY EXAM QUESTIONS

As you grade essay responses, are you looking for certain information, connections, analysis, or creativity of thought? Before grading essay responses, establish with your professor the criteria for grading. Write your own model response to the question to be sure that you have thought of all the important criteria.

Some kind of simple grading rubric would help you evaluate the exams. Decide with your professor what are the most important elements for each response. List them in a holistic rubric. (See Chapter 11.) For a question such as "What are the pros and cons of using a rational choice paradigm?" the rubric may include "a clear understanding of the rational choice paradigm" and "at least two advantages and two disadvantages listed and explained." This rubric may seem obvious, but writing it out will clarify grading. Writing the rubric may also help you recognize ambiguities in your question, allowing you to make clarifying revisions before you give the exam to your students.

As you grade essay responses, you may wonder what to do about mechanical errors. Remember that essay exams are written in a limited time and without revision. You can be charitable about small mechanical errors, but you should read carefully for understanding of important concepts, synthesis of ideas, and analysis of information. Second-language students and those who have learning disabilities may require some test-taking accommodations, such as longer time or the use of a dictionary. As John Bean says, read "demandingly at the macro level (thesis, organization, use of evidence), and forgivingly at the micro level (sentence structure, punctuation errors)."[11]

When you assess the responses, try the following strategies.[12]

- Don't look at students' names when reading the exams.

- Grade the exam one question at a time (all the responses to question 1, then all the responses to question 2, etc.). If more than one person is grading the exams, you may want to have grade-norming sessions in order to be sure that you are all grading by the same standards. (See Chapter 11.)

- Change the order of the exams each time you start on a new question. Don't be influenced by how a certain student did on question 2 when you are grading question 3.

- Try reading several exam responses before you start assigning grades. Find models of excellent, medium, and poor responses to "anchor" your grading. When you are confused about what grade to assign, refer to one of your models.

Essay exams are a good way to assess students' comprehension. Work with your professor to plan effective questions and evaluation methods. If possible and appropriate, teach students how to do well on essay tests. If you do so, the exams will truly do what they are meant to: give the students a chance to demonstrate their command of the material.

Teaching Tip: Guidelines for Doing Well on Essay Exams

Teaching your students the following guidelines will help them do well on essay exams. Think of some others that would specifically apply to your class.

- **Take time to understand the question.** Students need to read the question carefully and answer what has been asked.
- **Plan before writing.** Though time is obviously limited, taking a few minutes to jot down a scratch outline of the essay will save students time in the long run. As they make the outline, they can be sure that they are answering the question. They can write down main points to include so that they don't forget them later.
- **Don't summarize unless it's asked for.** Usually a good essay question will require original analysis, not a summary of facts or events.
- **Get the facts right.** Students should memorize important names, dates, formulas, and other facts that may be needed on the exam.
- **Budget time.** Teach students to look over the exam when they get it and briefly decide how much time to allocate to each question. They can then try to stay on schedule and not leave a major essay unfinished because of lack of time.

(continued)

> **Teaching Tip** *(continued)*
>
> - **Leave a few minutes for proofreading.** Reading over a response quickly, a student can insert words that have been left out or fix other errors that could influence the grader's comprehension.
>
> - **Use a format that makes comprehension easy.** Using headings and underlining key words could make the grader's task easier. Teach students to think about their audience in essay exams, as in all writing.

Research Papers

A research paper or term paper requires students to find information on a certain topic, read and understand that information, and then use the information to support a certain thesis in their paper. It is an excellent way for students to learn independently and to perform complex synthesis and analysis.

Such assignments are likely to fail, however, when assigned according to the "mystery model" described by Tom Romano.[13] Sometimes a teacher assigns the long paper at the beginning of the term and doesn't refer to it again until collecting the finished product at the end of the term. All the writing work of the paper remains a "mystery" for the student.

If students are not guided through the mystery in between when the assignment is given and when the paper is turned in, they often have no idea how to go about completing the paper. They might end up writing the paper in one all-night marathon on the eve of the due date, or they might even resort to plagiarism. Teachers can help students write better research papers by teaching research skills and the steps of the research process.

INTERMEDIATE ASSIGNMENTS FOR RESEARCH PAPERS

The following intermediate assignments could be submitted and reviewed on the way to the final research paper. Requiring these submissions would encourage students to get started early on their papers, but, more than that, these assignments allow you to give students feedback as they go along. With this guidance, students will learn how to write better papers in general and how to improve this paper specifically. Talk to your professor about assigning a few intermediate assignments such as those listed here.

- **Three possible topics for the paper.** In responding, you or the teacher could give guidance on which topic might work best.

- **A specific research question or a tentative thesis statement.** You could respond to these individually and/or look at some as a class to learn what an appropriately limited thesis is.

- **An annotated preliminary bibliography.** You can check to see if the student has enough sources and if the sources are appropriate and specific to the topic. You can also help students understand your discipline's documentation format before the final paper is submitted.

- **A tentative thesis and outline.** You can quickly check these to see if the paper's overall plan is logical and appropriate for the scope of the assignment.

- **A review of the literature.** Having to write about their sources forces students to start finding and reading sources early on. Also, writing such a review helps students to think about similarities and differences among their sources. They can group together sources that treat the subject in the same way and identify the disagreements among the various authors.

- **A research proposal or prospectus.** This assignment needs to be carefully designed to include all the information you and your professor need to determine if the research project is viable. Refer to discipline-specific requirements for professional or graduate proposals in your field for ideas on how to define the requirements for your class. Adapt those requirements so that they fit the needs of the particular class you teach. The proposal may include a rationale for the choice of topic, an explanation of the particular thesis, a survey of the proposed paper's structure, a review of the literature consulted, an outline, and a preliminary bibliography.

- **Copies of a rough draft for peer review.** Have students exchange their rough drafts. They could read the papers outside of class and then come back prepared to help each other improve their papers. A prepared list of questions to consider would guide this review. The reviewer could be required to write a detailed analysis of the draft to be graded. As part of the analysis, the reviewer could even check to make sure sources were used ethically. (See Chapter 13.)

- **A rough draft for TA review.** You could read over drafts of the paper and give comments for revision. If you do this, also grade the drafts so that students will submit carefully written papers for your review. Reading drafts that are essentially last-minute attempts at prewriting will just frustrate you without helping the student.

Requiring intermediate assignments that lead up to the final major paper will accomplish several purposes. The students will get started early so that they will have enough time to think through the topic, do thorough research, and write multiple drafts. And you will be able to guide the students' writing early in their processes, intervening at points when they can adjust their papers with minimal effort. Tracking the students' work throughout the research process will make plagiarism much less likely. But the most important reason for assigning intermediate writing assignments is that the students will learn much more about the topic and about writing as they complete the assignments.

TEACHING RESEARCH SKILLS

You cannot assume that students know how to do research. If possible, team up with a librarian to teach students how to find sources in appropriate databases in your particular subject area. You could hold a help session in a computer classroom to practice using data-search programs. Meeting students in the library, you could give them hands-on instruction in finding sources. Even just talking in class about how to solve common research problems can help eliminate some of the students' frustrations.

Undergraduate students often need help knowing how to read research articles that are written for a specialized audience of scholars in the field. Try bringing a sample article to class and reading it together. Explain the conventions controlling the format of the article. Discuss what kinds of information you are likely to find in each part. Science professors tell me they rarely read a research article from beginning to end. Instead they might read the abstract first, to see if the information is pertinent to their interest. If it is, then they will turn to the results sections, and perhaps next check the methodology. If the research merits further perusal, they will then examine the rest of the article. Talk to your students about effective ways to approach professional research in your discipline.

Depending on your students' level of experience, you may want to teach them how to appropriately summarize and paraphrase. Teach them how to use a variety of sources to support their points by reading model essays together. Sources can be used for a variety of purposes; help students to see these uses in their reading, as well as how to use sources appropriately in their writing

Be sure that students understand the specialized citation conventions in your discipline. Provide them with samples of citations and bibliography entries. You may want to take some class time to practice using your discipline's particular style guide.

Technology Tactics

The following online resources provided by Bedford/St. Martin's feature helpful tools for students conducting research and working on source-based writing.

- **The Bedford Researcher Online.** At <bedfordresearcher.com/tutorials .cfm>, students will find tutorials on conducting and refining Internet searches, evaluating online sources, and integrating source material into their writing. Students will also find an index of discipline-specific research links at <bedfordresearcher.com/links>.

- **Research and Documentation Online.** At <dianahacker.com/resdoc>, students will find guidelines and models for documenting print and online sources in MLA, APA, *Chicago,* and CBE styles; sample documented student papers; and annotated links to discipline-specific research sites.

PREPARING THE ASSIGNMENT AND GRADING RUBRIC

Because the research paper is a complex assignment, be sure that your instructions are clear and complete. Your criteria for grading need to be thorough and easily available to the students as they are working on the paper. Example 12.1 features an assignment sheet and grading rubric for a physical science research paper that shows the types of information you should give your students.

EXAMPLE 12.1. A Research Paper Assignment Sheet and Grading Rubric[i]

PS 100—RESEARCH PAPER
Description: You must submit a 3–5-page (1200–2000 word) paper on one of the suggested topics or the instructor-approved topic of your choosing.
Purpose: The paper is designed to develop your ability to use scientific reasoning skills and to explain your reasoning in writing. This assignment will give you an opportunity to thoroughly investigate a current scientific issue and use the concepts you are learning to come to a decision about it.
Format: The paper is to be typed, double spaced, on 8½" × 11" paper, with name and NetID# at the top of each page.
Due Dates: *No late work will be accepted.* Your first and second drafts are due in lab the weeks of Oct. 21 and Oct. 28, respectively. Your final paper must be turned in to your TA's box by 5:00 P.M. on Tues. Nov. 26. You are free to turn your work in early if your holiday plans conflict with the deadline.
Grading: The paper is worth 50 points. You will be graded primarily on the correctness and completeness of your science and your ability to defend your position. The evaluation criteria are listed below. Graded papers can be picked up in your recitation sections. Any questions about grading should be addressed to your TA. All grading questions must be resolved before Dec. 12.
Plagiarism: Taking credit for anyone else's words or ideas is plagiarism. Plagiarism includes not only turning in a paper partially or completely written by someone else, but also paraphrasing or summarizing someone else's work, or using someone else's idea without giving them credit. Plagiarism will not be tolerated. Inadvertent plagiarism (failing to properly cite all sources, wholesale paraphrasing, etc.) will be severely penalized. Deliberate plagiarism will result in a failing grade, and the student will be reported to the honor code office.

Evaluation criteria	
Prewriting: 10 pts	**Description**
Thesis: 1.5 pts Annotated bibliography: 1.5 pts Peer review: 4 pts Draft: 3 pts	Points will be awarded for doing the appropriate prewriting tasks well and on time. You will get no points if the task is not completed on time. You will get partial points if you turn in incomplete or poor-quality work. *(continued)*

---

[i]Thanks to Jeanette Lawler, Department of Physics and Astronomy, Brigham Young University.

EXAMPLE 12.1. *(continued)*

Content: 23 pts	Description
Choice of references: 3 pts	Points will be awarded for correct science and a well-reasoned paper. You should make sure you are using reputable peer-reviewed sources. Where appropriate, opposing views should be represented. *Be cautious with Web sources.*
Quality of scientific evidence: 10 pts	This is a science paper. You need to make sure it contains good quality scientific evidence. You will lose points if your science is incomplete or incorrect.
Use of supporting evidence: 10 pts	You need to support your thesis with evidence. Your reasoning should be sound and convincing. There should be no logical fallacies.
Organization: 12 pts	**Description**
Clear, consistent thesis: 4 pts	Your thesis should be clearly stated in the introduction, and your paper should be organized around supporting the thesis. You should not get sidetracked by other ideas.
Interesting to read: 4 pts	The topic should be interesting to you, and your paper should convey that interest. The tone and style should be honest, not stiff and formal. Quoted material should be integrated into your own sentences and ideas. You should be stating your own ideas, not simply summarizing someone else's.
Clarity of ideas: 4 pts	Sentences and paragraphs should be well organized around central ideas. There should be clear transitions between ideas. The grader shouldn't have any "Wait! What are you talking about?" moments.
English: 5 pts	**Description**
Correctness: 5 pts	You will lose points for grammar, punctuation, and spelling mistakes. *Proofread your paper carefully.*

Extended research projects can be an excellent learning experience for your students. Providing feedback at each step of the project will help students work toward a substantive final product. Students often require overt instruction in specialized skills, such as finding and reading sources and integrating borrowed information. Preparing clear instructions and a grading rubric will help students meet the professor's expectations. Do what you can as a TA to help students understand how to write effective research papers in your field.

Collaborative Writing Projects

In many professions, writing in teams or groups is the norm. When preparing students for those professions, professors may give collaborative assignments as a context for teaching team-writing skills. Collaborative papers also allow the professor to assign writing in very large classes while limiting the number of papers to be graded.

Simply dividing the class and telling the students to write a paper in groups is asking for trouble, however. Sometimes one good student takes on all the work of completing the paper while others in the group contribute little. Other groups might argue over what to do and how to do it. The following are some suggestions for designing a collaborative writing assignment so that it will be more likely to succeed.

- **Teach collaborative writing strategies.** Give a detailed assignment, with a clear sequence of steps leading to the final product.

- **Explain ways to divide the work equitably.** One group member might be the "team leader," and each of the other members might research two different sources and prepare notes to be shared. All but one could be assigned to draft a section of the report, while that last person is responsible for putting all the drafts together into a coherent whole. Make sure that each member is doing his or her fair share of work.

- **Include peer review of drafts among the groups.** On a given day, have each group bring a good draft of their collaborative project. Exchange papers and have each group evaluate another group's paper, using a prepared set of questions to guide them. A note-taker can write down their reactions to the paper. The resulting comments will help the authors of the paper to revise more effectively. Doing the analysis will also help the group to see the concerns in their own paper when they return to it.

- **Arrange for group meetings.** Set aside time in class or outside of class to check on the groups' progress.

- **Have students evaluate each other's performance.** One idea is to have the students divide a total of 100 points among the group members, but not allow them to give an equal number to each participant. This way they have to think about who contributed the most and the least. Use such evaluations when determining the groups' grades.

Collaborative assignments can teach important skills in project management and teamwork. Teaching students methods of completing the project as a group is an important part of helping them with this kind of writing.

Technology Tactics

Electronic communication can enhance students' work on collaborative projects.

- **Email.** Students can email each other to discuss the project. They can attach their drafts to the email so that the group can review them and insert their comments and revisions. Compiling the final group document is much easier because the digital copies can easily be combined into one, for final revision.

- **Class Web site.** Commercially prepared class Web site programs such as Blackboard have many tools that could benefit collaborative projects. In Blackboard, you can set up specially designated "groups." These groups can then communicate easily either to all in the group or to selected members. They can save the drafts of their individual contributions to a group drop box, where group members can collect them and comment on them. They can even set up a synchronous chat room. For example, a group might decide they will chat at 10:00 P.M. on Monday night. Then they all meet in the chat room to discuss their project, even though they are miles apart physically.

- **Editing functions.** As students review each others' papers, they can use the "track changes" function available in most word-processing programs to show the changes they make in each others' papers. If the group agrees with the changes, they can be applied to the document with the click of a button. They can also use the "insert comments" function (also available in most programs) to include their ideas for the draft.

Conclusion

Each writing assignment has specific elements to be considered. As you and the professor make these assignments, think about ways to teach skills needed to succeed in the assignment and ways to guide the students' writing through the process. Consider the needs of the students and the purposes of the assignment when preparing essay exams, and when assigning research papers and collaborative projects. If you do, you can teach valuable skills that students will use long after finishing your class.

> ### *Chapter Checklist*
>
> ☐ Essay exam questions must be carefully designed to be sure that the responses will actually demonstrate the kind of understanding you are looking for. Grading these responses can be more consistent and fair if certain guidelines are followed.
>
> ☐ Research papers are complex assignments. Student writing will be improved if you teach them the skills they need and require intermediate assignments to be submitted leading up to the final paper.
>
> ☐ Collaborative writing assignments may be used to teach skills necessary to working as a team in the workplace.

Applications to Your Own Situation

1. Find an essay question from your discipline. Analyze its effectiveness. How could it be improved?

2. Write a good response to an essay question you will be grading. Did the question confuse you as you tried to answer it? How could the question be clearer?

3. If you will be grading essay questions for the class you TA, use the suggestions in the chapter to determine an effective means of doing the grading.

4. Have you ever been in a class where the "mystery model" was employed for assigning a research paper? As a student, how did you respond to that? How did other students handle the situation?

5. If a research paper is required for the class you TA, work with your professor to determine ways to guide the students through the research process.

6. What intermediate assignments might help the students to write the research paper?

7. What has been your experience with collaborative writing projects? What differences do you see between writing collaboratively as students and doing collaborative work on the job, as professionals?

8. If your class will be doing a collaborative project, what are some guidelines you and your professor could provide that would make the project go more smoothly?

9. Devise a way for students to fairly evaluate each others' work on a collaborative project.

Working with Your Professor

1. Ask your professor for models of good papers—both to share with students and for you to use as grading guides. This way you can be sure you understand the conventions of the kinds of papers your students will write.

2. Be sure you and your professor have the same understanding of the purpose and conventions of each assignment.
3. Work with your professor to design good essay questions and clear criteria for grading them.
4. Work with your professor to plan intermediate assignments leading up to a final research paper.
5. Work with your professor to prepare students well for collaborative assignments.

CHAPTER 13

Plagiarism and Other Grading-Related Concerns

*"The lessons I learned that were most important were
the ones that hurt my feelings."*

—Robert Stone

In this chapter you will learn

■ strategies for dealing effectively with plagiarism, grade disputes, appeals to pity, and procrastinating students.

In teaching, as in life, all does not go smoothly. This chapter discusses several problems TAs sometimes encounter, such as plagiarism, grade disputes, appeals to pity, and procrastinating students, and it offers a variety of strategies for responding to such problems.

Plagiarism

Thanks to technology, plagiarising is easier than ever. Students need not go to the trouble of "borrowing" papers from friends anymore. They can simply copy sections from Web sites and paste them directly into their papers without indicating the source. Or they can even purchase entire papers through numerous "paper mill" Web sites. As a TA you need to be aware of plagiarism, how to avoid it, how to detect it, and what to do when you find it.

WHAT IS PLAGIARISM?

Plagiarism is simply the theft of ideas, either in the exact language of the original or as a paraphrase. Sometimes students do this inadvertently. For example, someone may not understand that a source must be cited even when the ideas borrowed have been restated in a paraphrase. At other times, a student may knowingly copy material from another source or even submit a paper written by someone else. Sometimes students do this out of desperation, and sometimes they do it simply to avoid work. In any case, plagiarism cannot be allowed.

DISCOURAGING PLAGIARISM

In an article in *The Chronicle of Higher Education,* Rebecca Moore Howard[1] suggests that the way instructors assign and respond to student writing can discourage the practice of plagiarism. To make plagiarism less likely in your classes, try the following strategies.

- **Assign meaningful writing assignments.** Writing assignments should grow specifically out of the context of the class and, as Howard explains, respond to the "needs and interests of the students in a particular section of the class."[2] This would not only make the students more interested in completing the assignment, but it would also make it more difficult to find a ready-made paper that would fit the specificity of the assignment.

- **Monitor students' progress on the paper.** If you ask for intermediate assignments—such as a thesis statement, outline, or annotated bibliography—leading up to the final draft, students will be guided in preparing the paper and feel more confident that they can complete the assignment. (See Chapter 12.) Also, they will find that doing all the preparatory assignments from a stolen, purchased, or borrowed paper would be more work than actually writing the paper from scratch themselves.

- **Respond respectfully to student writing.** If students know that you will read all their written work carefully and respectfully, they will want to write for you, and they will know that you will probably recognize any attempts at plagiarism.

- **Teach the appropriate conventions for documentation.** Make sure students understand that the purpose of research is to support their own carefully formed argument.

- **Make your policies clear.** In the class syllabus and/or on the assignment sheet, define plagiarism for students and provide clear guidelines for your professor's, the department's, or school's policies on plagiarism. Let students know the penalties for plagiarism.

DETECTING PLAGIARISM

While good teaching can prevent plagiarism, as a TA you still need to be alert to the possibility that students may plagiarize. Robert A. Harris offers a number of ways to detect plagiarism.[3]

- **Look for obvious clues.** Obvious signs of plagiarism include lack of citations, references to material not included in the text, signs of datedness, and URLs that are no longer available. Sometimes the paper just looks familiar; maybe you've had it submitted before, or you've read the source from which it was plagiarized.

- **Look for inconsistent style.** If the paper is much better written than anything else this student has submitted, it may not be original. Sometimes some parts of the paper are much better written than the rest because those pieces have come from another source.

- **Check local sources.** See if your professor or department keeps files of papers written in the past for this class. Thumb through papers on topics or in response to assignments similar to yours. Compare your batch of papers to those in the file, looking for similar-sounding titles or thesis statements.

- **Check for the paper online, using a search engine.** Sometimes just searching for a phrase in the paper will lead to the original source.

CONFRONTING PLAGIARISM

As a TA, it is always your responsibility to alert your professor of your suspicions. However, both you and your professor should be aware that inadvertent plagiarism should be treated differently from intentional plagiarism.

- **Inadvertent plagiarism.** Recognize that a novice writer may not understand what constitutes plagiarism or may not understand documentation conventions. An international student may have different cultural expectations regarding the use of sources. In such cases, the instructor's primary responsibility would be to teach the student the skills needed and ask that the student rewrite the paper, demonstrating clear understanding of proper documentation.

- **Intentional plagiarism.** Have clear policies in place for dealing with intentionally deceptive plagiarism. Depending on the severity of the case, your professor may want to give the plagiarized paper an *F* grade or give the student a failing grade for the class. Find out if your school has a central office where you can report the plagiarism so that students who plagiarize repeatedly can be monitored. If plagiarism is a common practice for a student, he or she may be expelled from school. If this occurs, remember that it is *not your fault:* it is the student's.

Technology Tactics

The following online resource provided by Bedford/St. Martin's features helpful resources and information for instructors concerned about plagiarism.

- **The Bedford/St. Martin's Workshop on Plagiarism.** This site, <bedfordstmartins.com/plagiarism>, features downloadable handouts on plagiarism for students and instructors, information on how to use writing portfolios, online discussion forums to avoid plagiarism, links to full-text articles about plagiarism and the Internet, and links to other Bedford/St. Martin's workshops and online professional resources.

As discussed in Chapter 12, Bedford/St. Martin's offers helpful online resources for students conducting research and working on source-based writing.

Grade Disputes

"You've made a mistake. I never get anything lower than an *A*." Sometimes a student has an inflated opinion of his or her abilities. Sometimes he or she really has received only *A*s. But you can't change the grade to match the student's past experience; you have to grade his or her work as it stands—today—against the agreed-upon criteria. Grades are very important to students, so you should be careful not to trivialize their concerns. Listen respectfully to them and try to explain how they can do better. If a student is still dissatisfied, encourage the student to take his or her paper to the professor responsible for the class for another reading, if the professor is willing. The *Chicago Handbook for Teachers* explains, "You should not feel that a student who appeals your grade is undermining your authority. The professor is the ultimate authority, and it is reasonable for students to expect a hearing from him or her."[4]

You and your professor should work out your own strategy for dealing with grade disputes. The following is a three-step method that can work well.

1.   Point out that you are evaluating the student's work in the present class, not the student's past experience. Explain that you will be happy to discuss the paper so that he or she can do better next time. If the student still thinks the grade does not reflect the quality of the paper, move to the next step.

2.   Ask the student to write down reasons why the paper deserves a higher grade, but only after reviewing his or her paper, your comments, and the grading rubric carefully. Ask the student to write a persuasive argument for changing the paper's grade.

3.   Discuss the paper's grade only after the student has written the analysis. Together with the professor, you can evaluate the student's reasons for requesting the grade change and take appropriate action.

Appeals to Pity

"But I worked *so* hard!" This appeal can be touching because some students do try very hard, only to find that the paper does not reflect the intensity of their work. Still, you are not evaluating the amount of work that goes into the paper, only the quality of the final product. Therefore, the way to respond to this appeal is to help the student improve the quality of his or her paper. Offer to help the student in the planning stages of the next paper. Early in the writing process, you could help the student to come up with a good thesis and structure and find good support. Also suggest that the student bring early drafts to you during your office hours for review. (See Chapter 8.) Help the student by teaching him or her strategies that will lead to a better paper.

Teaching Tip: Advice from Others on Grading Questions

Be aware of possible problems that could arise concerning grading, and make a plan with your professor for dealing with them. When a situation you haven't thought of comes up, don't be afraid talk to ask your professor and others in your department or school for advice on dealing with the problem. Teaching is learning, and your professors and fellow TAs will respect your efforts to solve a difficult situation. Share your findings. Your solution may even address a problem that one of your colleagues has been struggling with.

Procrastinating Students

"If you can just give me another day/week/month/semester, this will be perfect." Some students will delay submitting a paper because they know it is not perfect, and they will accept only perfection. Some students think they are just too busy to finish the paper. Either way, you're doing them no favor by extending the deadline. Try the following strategies to avoid such a situation or to deal with one if it ever arises.

- Determine with your professor a firm late paper policy, with significant penalties, and hold to it.
- Encourage your professor to publish the late-paper policy in the course syllabus and/or assignment sheets. Make sure the students know it will be enforced.
- If a student has a true emergency—a serious illness, death in the family, or serious injury—quietly try to corroborate the student's story and, if it is true, give that deserving soul a break. But don't let that information get around.

Conclusion

Dealing with plagiarism and students' grade concerns are among the most difficult things you will do as a TA. It is easy to get caught up in personal considerations, worrying about a student's emotional reaction to the punishment, the assignment, the grade, or you. However, academic integrity and fairness must overrule emotion.

Remember that a student who is punished for committing intentional plagiarism effectively brought that punishment upon him- or herself. You did not break the rules; the student did. Remember that the grade you assign is a powerful symbol to the student, the school, and future employers. The grade must accurately reflect the quality of the student's work, and poor-quality work should be given a poor grade.

Chapter Checklist

☐ Try to prevent plagiarism by carefully designing your writing assignments and by teaching documentation skills thoroughly.

(continued)

Chapter Checklist (continued)

☐ When you suspect plagiarism, tell your professor and work with him or her to handle the situation appropriately. If the plagiarism seems to come from a lack of understanding, teach the student the necessary skills and perhaps allow a second chance. If the student has plagiarized intentionally, your professor—or the school—will need to take punitive actions.

☐ Have a plan in place for dealing with students who challenge their grades.

☐ Don't change a grade for pity's sake. Instead, offer to help the student improve his or her writing skills so that he or she will earn a better grade next time.

☐ Have a firm late-paper policy in place. Make exceptions only for *true* emergencies.

Applications to Your Own Situation

1. Familiarize yourself with your school's honor code or statement on academic honesty or plagiarism. Be sure you understand the school's definitions of plagiarism and the prescribed methods for dealing with it.
2. Review the class syllabus to see if intermediate assignments could be added as a means of deterring plagiarism.
3. Find ways to teach the documentation conventions of your discipline so that students will not unintentionally plagiarize. (See the Technology Tactics box on p. 129.)
4. Brainstorm a list of grading-related problems not discussed in this chapter that might come up. Think of possible ways to deal with the problems.

Working with Your Professor

1. Discuss a scenario in which you suspect a student has committed plagiarism. Determine what type of evidence your professor would want as proof and how he or she would determine whether the plagiarism was inadvertent or intentional.
2. Discuss specific grading-related concerns that your professor has dealt with in the past. What advice can he or she give you about these types of situations? If necessary, use Application 4 as a basis for your discussion.
3. Work with your professor to draft policy statements on plagiarism, grade disputes, and late papers and publish them in the class syllabus, assignment sheets, or in a stand-alone handout.

CHAPTER 14

Maintaining Professionalism

"The secret of education is respecting the pupil."

—Ralph Waldo Emerson

In this chapter you will learn

- how to help students who lack basic writing skills.
- about learning disabilities and how to advise students who may have them.
- ways to help international students with writing.
- how to respond if students share emotional problems with you.
- tips for avoiding bias.
- how to avoid situations that could be construed as sexual harassment.

In the course you are TAing, you are likely to address a variety of problems that do not directly relate to grading. Some students come to your class with individual concerns that will inhibit their ability to write well or learn. Some students will have other concerns requiring assistance. Some situations are just inherently problematic. The ideas contained in this chapter should not be considered as prescriptions or formulas for responding to such situations. Instead, these discussions might alert you to the kinds of problems you may face and give you a few suggestions for dealing with such concerns. Always discuss problems with your professor as they arise. Together you can determine good ways of responding to them.

Students Lacking Basic Writing Skills

You may find that some students in your class simply lack good writing skills. Because you are a TA for a subject-specific course, you probably do not have the time to teach these students basic usage. However, there are some simple ways to support the students in improving their skills.

- Show the students how to use a writing handbook, and encourage them to invest in one and study it. (See the Bibliography for a list of good handbooks.)

- If your school has a writing center, refer students there for extra help. Because writing-center tutors are trained to teach skills, not "fix" papers, they will not proofread and edit a draft. However, if students ask for help learning a certain skill (for example, how to avoid fragments), the tutors will teach the skill in the context of the students' own writing.

- Suggest that students find a qualified English tutor to work with them individually on achieving college-level writing skills.

Technology Tactics

The following online resources provided by Bedford/St. Martin's feature free interactive grammar exercises. These sites allow students to practice grammar and usage skills in a noncompetitive, self-paced environment. The exercises give instant feedback and instruction to help students reinforce their understanding of writing-related concepts. Such exercises are no substitute for applying concepts in the context of students' papers, but these exercises can help students to clarify certain usage conventions.

- **Exercise Central.** At <bedfordstmartins.com/exercisecentral>, students will find the largest collection of editing exercises—with automatic feedback—available online that provide practice for mastering the skills of editing grammar, style, punctuation, and mechanics.
- **The Bedford Handbook Online.** At <dianahacker.com/bedhandbook>, students will find electronic exercises for grammar, research, and writing that allow them to practice essential skills in an interactive environment. More than 1,000 items with feedback after each item reinforce key grammatical and writing-related concepts.

Students with Learning Disabilities

Learning disabilities are difficult to define, and even more difficult to diagnose. However, as a TA, you need to realize that students may have some "central nervous sytem dysfunction"[1] that interferes with their ability to read or write. Students may know this already and be working with your school's accessibility services (or equivalent) to accommodate their differences. With the authorization of accessibility services, these students may ask that legitimate accommodations be made. For example, they may need longer time for an in-class essay, or they may need to listen to texts on tape rather than read them. With your professor's approval, give these students the accommodations they need. However, hold them to as high a standard as the rest of the class for their finished work.

If a student seems to be achieving at a lower level on tests and papers than you would expect from his or her performance orally and when there seems to be no evident condition that would cause that underachievement, you might suspect the presence of some kind of learning disability.[2] Discuss with the professor the possibility that the student be tested by accessibility services to determine if a learning disability does exist. Diagnosis and learning accommodation strategies could help a student with a learning disability succeed academically.

International Students (Nonnative Speakers of English)

International students have a particularly tough time with writing assignments. In addition to the obvious difficulties of not being completely fluent in English, international students often have differing cultural and social expectations and miss the network of family and friends that they may have relied on at home. The school system in their home country may be very different, and simply not understanding the American academic system can be a deterrent to learning.[3]

Obviously, these students have varying degrees of facility with the English language. Because they may not fully understand verbal instructions, it is especially important to provide written assignment descriptions when international students are in your class. Encourage your professor to create very clear, written assignment explanations so that students not fluent in English can study the requirements on their own with the help of a dictionary. If the professor does not create such a document, perhaps you could do so with his or her permission. To accompany the written explanation, provide model papers that demonstrate clearly the expectations for the assignment. These resources will help all your students, but they are especially useful to international students for whom the expectations of American academic writing may be new.[4]

Of all the students in your class, international students will probably be most likely to ask for your help with surface-level writing concerns. Remember, though, that you are a teacher, not an editor. Encourage your international students to study a handbook or find a tutor. You may also want to refer students to the online grammar resources described in the Technology Tactics box on p. 134. As with all your students, determine the most relevant skill a particular student needs to know in a particular paper, and then teach it.

Perhaps one of the most important things to teach international students is that basic assumptions about writing vary from culture to culture. Robert B. Kaplan, a pioneering researcher into cultural differences regarding writing, explains that there are markedly different assumptions about "Who writes what to whom, how, when, where, and to what end."[5] Some cultures do not assume that students have the right to express original ideas. Different cultures have different ideas about the most effective ways to organize an argument or what constitutes good evidence. Good writing in some cultures may zigzag from one idea to another or follow a much more circular structure, with the thesis appearing near the end of the paper. Kaplan's cultural thought pattern "doodles," shown in Figure 14.1, demonstrate the differing writing structures found in various cultures.[6]

Because of these differences, international students often need instruction in the linear method of organization expected in American academic writing. Show them how we expect a thesis statement in the introduction and how everything in the paper follows directly from that thesis. Explain how topic sentences

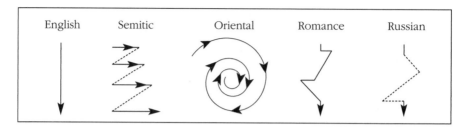

Figure 14.1. Kaplan's Cultural Thought Pattern "Doodles"

control the content of each paragraph. You might use highlighters to show how each part of the thesis is developed in consecutive sections of the paper. Be careful not to imply that the American way of writing is the only "right" way, but simply explain that this is the way Americans write.

You can address international students' writing concerns in one-on-one conferences. (See Chapter 8.) Because of differing cultural expectations, however, international students may not understand how to interact in such a setting. In many cultures students would never think to disagree with their teachers. If you say, "I think you should do this," or "This is what you are trying to say," international students may be even more likely than other students to simply agree with you. Take the time to explicitly discuss the expectations for student contribution in a conference situation. Let the students know you expect them to speak freely about their ideas and that you want to know what they are thinking.[7] Use open-ended questions to encourage students to contribute.

Teaching Tip: Open-Ended Questions

When conferencing with ESL students, it is especially important to phrase your questions so that there is no expectation of a single correct answer. As discussed in Chapter 8, use open-ended questions that allow students to think creatively about how to express their own ideas. Sometimes it is hard to compose truly open-ended questions that do not lead students to a particular answer you know you want. One key is to keep the attitude of respect for the student. Don't assume that you automatically know what is best for him or her. Expect the student to surprise you with better ideas than you would have thought of. Following are a few suggestions for open-ended questions you could use in conferences with ESL students.

- "Tell me about what you are trying to accomplish with this paper."
- "Explain to me your reasons for believing X."
- "Show me your organizational plan in outline form."
- "Talk me through the connections between the various sections in your paper. Describe to me how parts A, B, and C support your thesis and connect to each other."
- "Every paragraph should have a topic sentence stating the main purpose

of that paragraph. Use this highlighter to mark the topic sentence for this paragraph. Explain how all the information in the paragraph ties together."

- "Is this sentence in your paper in active or passive voice? Which do you think would work best in this case?" (See p. 59 for more on active and passive voice.)

Most important, treat international students naturally. Rik Andes, an English as a Second Language (ESL) instructor, says, "Have fun with ESL students. Learning a foreign language is hard enough—treat the situation carefully and help them discover the correct patterns in an enjoyable way."[8] Remember to respect these students. It takes great courage and ability to study in a foreign country in an unfamiliar language. These brave and bright students deserve the extra guidance you can provide, but remember to hold international students to the same high standards you expect from your other students.

Students with Emotional Problems

Sometimes students will share personal concerns in a writing assignment or a writing conference. These students trust you, and you should respond with a concern worthy of that trust. However, you are *not* in a position to offer professional counseling to those in need of it. These situations require great sensitivity as well as professionalism.

Composition professor Marilyn J. Valentino suggests the following guidelines for dealing with students who have emotional problems.[9]

- Learn about your legal responsibilities and the support available at your school and in your community.
- Keep the contact information for support services handy so that you can refer students in need there.
- Ask questions to be sure you understand what the student is discussing. Don't jump to conclusions.
- Don't keep the concern to yourself. As a TA, be sure to tell the professor of all such problems. With his or her cooperation, you may both want to talk the problem over with a professional.
- Remember that you are a teacher, not a counselor or even a buddy. Remain a professional. Don't think you can "rescue" anyone. Valentino suggests using questions such as "Is there someone you trust whom you can talk to about this?" "Are you talking to anyone else about the problem you are having?" or "How would you want to solve this?"[10]
- You can also say, "I don't have the authority [experience, background] to help you, but I can give you the number of the campus counselor so that you can make an appointment to talk with someone. Or would you like me to call the counseling center or walk over with you now?"[11]

Avoiding Bias

Be careful not to let gender-based stereotypes influence your dealings with students. For example, don't assume that a woman is likely to have trouble with computational skills or that a man is likely to misunderstand the emotional import of a novel. Elizabeth Birmingham studied male and female graders, comparing how they responded to male and female students' papers. She found that when responding to male students, male TAs were 25 percent more likely to offer praise than criticism. In contrast, female students received twice as much criticism as praise from male TAs. The male TAs were more likely to ask female students questions that challenged their mental abilities, such as "So, what's your point?"; "I don't get it"; and "In other words, I'm confused."[12] In contrast, the male TAs asked male students questions that focused more on lack of effort than lack of ability, such as "You're a good writer. I expected more of you."[13] Be sure that in your teaching and your grading, you treat both male and female students with equal respect.

Similarly, be sure that you avoid bias toward or against anyone on the basis of race, religion, sexuality, national origin, political affiliation, or any other distinction. Evaluate papers objectively based on the predetermined criteria you and your professor have set up. In your comments, keep the focus on the craft of writing, the development of the ideas, the structure of the paper, and the clarity of sentences. Never write a comment on a paper that could be construed as a personal attack.

Avoiding Sexual Harassment

Sexual harassment is a very real concern on today's campuses. Professors and TAs need to be especially careful that their dealings with students remain unequivocally on a professional level. Be sure that you are aware of your school's policies on this issue. *The Chicago Handbook for Teachers* offers the following good advice.[14]

- Maintain a professional distance from your students.
- Never become romantically involved with one of your students. The line between friendly behavior and what might be considered impropriety or sexual harassment is a fine one, but you should never cross or even approach it.
- Avoid meeting students alone in your home or theirs.
- Avoid unusual physical contact.
- Make sure not to make comments or use language that might be interpreted as flirtatious or provocative.
- When having one-on-one conferences with a student, always keep your meeting space's door open.

Conclusion

With the suggestions listed here, your professor's help, and your own good sense, you will be able to find sensible ways to handle the difficult situations that may arise. If one overall principle could guide you through any problem, it probably would be "respect the student." Always remember that the student is a person, just like you. Respect the student as a person and do what you can to help the student learn in your class.

Chapter Checklist

☐ Suggest that students with poor writing skills seek further individual help from the writing center or personal tutors. Suggest that students invest in a writing handbook.

☐ With your professor's support, be willing to make appropriate accommodations for students with learning disabilities.

☐ Be understanding of the challenges facing nonnative speakers of English. Be sure that expectations for assignments are clear.

☐ If students share emotional concerns with you, be respectful and kind. Refer them to the school counseling center for professional help.

☐ Treat all students equally, regardless of gender, race, religion, sexuality, national origin, political affiliation, or any other distinction.

☐ Maintain a professional distance with all students. Stay well away from behavior that could be interpreted as sexual harassment.

☐ Remember that each student is an important individual who deserves to be treated fairly and with respect.

Applications to Your Own Situation

1. Be aware of campus resources that can assist you and your students with problems such as those discussed in this chapter. Find the addresses and numbers of the various support services on your campus—the writing center, the accessibility services center, the center for international students, and the counseling center—and keep a list of contact information for these services handy.

2. After grading a set of papers, divide the papers by gender and check to see if you responded to both men and women in the same ways. Also scan through your responses to check for other forms of bias. Be sure that your responses focus objectively on helping students improve their writing without casting aspersions on their beliefs.

3. Familiarize yourself with your school's guidelines for avoiding sexual harassment. Be sure that you follow the guidelines carefully.

Working with Your Professor

1. Ask your professor about campus resources for helping students with particular challenges. Ask your professor if he or she has ever had to deal with a difficult situation. How did your professor handle it, and what kind of advice can he or she provide?
2. If you suspect a student may have an undiagnosed learning disability, be sure to discuss this with your professor before making recommendations to the student. Discuss difficult situations with your professor as they arise.
3. Discuss with your professor ways to make the assignment expectations particularly clear for international students. Share with your professor your understanding of problems an international student may be facing in the class.
4. If a student shares a serious emotional concern with you, discuss it sensitively with your professor. He or she may have a better insight into how to respond to the concern.

CHAPTER 15

Help! How Can I Do All This?

"Sometimes it helps to know that I just can't do it all. One step at a time is all that's possible—even when those steps are taken on the run."

—Anne W. Schaef

In this chapter you will learn

- time-saving techniques for teaching and evaluating writing.
- practical advice from experienced writing teachers.

When TAs or professors talk about teaching Writing Across the Curriculum, the first concern is almost always "How do I make time for it?" Faced with stacks of papers or exams to read, who wouldn't want to know immediately how to do all that grading more quickly? Teaching, responding to, and evaluating writing does take time. Lots of it. But you can use that time more efficiently. This chapter will review time-saving strategies already discussed in this book as well offer other tips for grading efficiently.

A Review of Time-Saving Tips

Many of the most effective ways to save time have already been discussed in this book. If you and your professor take the time to prepare students to write, the students are more likely to write good papers. And good papers are easier (and more fun) to read. The following are some reminders of the techniques you have learned already, with explanations of how they will help you to use your time more efficiently.

- **Use Writing-to-Learn assignments to encourage careful thought on the subject before and during writing.** These assignments usually do not need grades, only an audience. If at the end of class students write for five minutes on what questions they still have, you need not comment on these at all. Just skim through them, check for completion, make notes on what the common questions were, and convey those questions to your professor so that he or she can start the next lecture with a clarification of any confusing points. Students could also, in pairs or small groups, read what each other has written. There are many ways to give students an audience without having to comment on or grade a piece of writing. (See Chapter 2.)

- **Have students write more than you grade.** For example, students could write a weekly mini-essay, but you would select at random and grade only five of them. On another kind of assignment, you might collect the writing only at random times. One faculty member I know has students submit a short essay every week in response to a prompt. She collects the essays but doesn't grade them. One of the questions on the final exam matches one of the weekly writing prompts, but the students have no idea which one until they come to the exam. At the final exam, the professor passes back the weekly essays, the students staple the appropriate one to the exam, and she grades it as part of the final. (See Chapter 2.)

- **Teach students appropriate ways to write in their discipline.** Help them to understand the conventions you expect them to know, and their papers will be easier to read and evaluate. (See Chapter 2.)

- **Save time by designing good assignments.** If the writing assignments are designed to be meaningful in the context of the course, and if they are written clearly, students are less likely to be confused about what they are to do and will need less personal direction. (See Chapter 3.)

- **Save time by guiding students' writing processes.** If you have intermediate assignments such as submitting topics, thesis statements, annotated bibliographies, and so forth, the final papers will be better and easier to read. Also, these intermediate assignments are short and take little time to respond to, but the feedback comes at a time when it can most help the students to learn. Then, when you do the summative evaluation of the final paper, you can just assign a grade with only a few comments. (See Chapters 3–7.)

- **Use class time to teach writing skills.** Show models of good thesis statements and discuss them. Show models of good reviews of the literature and discuss them. Five minutes of explanation in class can save thirty minutes of writing individual comments on student papers. (See Chapter 9.)

- **Have students conduct peer reviews of drafts.** If you teach the students to conduct peer reviews and give them good guidelines, the students will receive valuable feedback that you don't have to provide. The peer review can occur in or out of class, or even online. (See Chapter 5.)

- **Save time by referring students to the writing center.** Most schools have some sort of drop-in writing center where students can bring their papers for review. The tutors there are trained to help with writing, though they may not have the subject-specific expertise that you have. Send students there for help with organization, focus, paragraphing, transitions, and the like. The tutors will help students learn to recognize and correct surfaces errors but will not edit students' papers. To help the tutor better understand the purpose and requirements of an assignment, remind students to bring copies of their assignment sheets or syllabi with them to the writing center. (See Chapter 5.)

■ **Remember that less is more in responding to papers.** Two or three comments a page is all that most students can work with. Choose your battles: Comment on the most important things. (See Chapter 10.)

■ **Clarify your grading criteria to make evaluation easier.** The grading criteria will help students to write better, and the grading rubric will help you to grade more efficiently. By checking off a grading rubric, you can give students a lot of specific feedback, while taking very little time. Also, you and your fellow graders will be more consistent in your evaluation (especially if you have practiced grade norming), and that will take away some of the worry of evaluation, which makes grading take longer. (See Chapter 11.)

■ **Recognize the difference between formative and summative comments.** Papers that will be revised are in a formative stage. You should give more feedback on these to help the student with revision. If you are reading the final draft at the end of the semester, however, you probably do not need to spend as much time on detailed comments. You can give the paper a summative grade, with some explanation for that grade (including a completed grading sheet). (See Chapter 11.)

■ **Use self- or peer evaluation of writing occasionally.** Be sure to prepare the evaluators well to do this. When students evaluate their own and others' writing, many of the most obvious problems are identified and improved without taking any of your time. As an added benefit, students learn what the grading criteria are, they understand your comments on the final draft better, and your comments can be briefer. (See Chapter 11.)

■ **Prepare your students to write in specialized genres.** Making the effort to explain to your class the specialized expectations for the particular kinds of writing they are to do will save you much time when responding to and evaluating the writing they turn in. Rather than writing "An abstract is a summary, not an introduction" fifty times, you need only spend five minutes explaining that distinction to the whole class. (See Chapter 12.)

■ **Set up procedures for dealing with commonly occurring concerns.** If you are prepared for various problems that may arise, you will not spend so much time or emotional energy deciding what to do. Just being aware of likely concerns and various strategies for resolving them will save you time and anxiety. (See Chapters 13–14.)

■ **Use technological resources to streamline your teaching and responding.** Many technological tools have the net effect of saving time. Posting assignment instructions on the class Web site saves you from having to find extra copies for students who lose their own. Virtual peer-response groups can save class time by having students evaluate each other's writing outside of class. Referring students to a reliable Web resource saves class and one-on-one meeting time and also encourages self-directed study. Many teachers find that responding to papers electronically takes less time than pen-and-paper responses. (See the Technology Tactics box in each chapter.)

Practical Advice from Experienced Writing Teachers

The strategies you have learned will help you to use your time effectively. In addition, here are some matter-of-fact methods for responding and evaluating quickly. The following tips have been collected from many experienced writing teachers.

- **Allow only so many minutes per paper you grade.** Determine how many papers you can read in an hour, then divide your papers into hour's-worth stacks. Read a stack, take a break, and then start the next hour's stack.

- **Respond more thoroughly to the first paper the students submit, and be very rigorous on that paper's evaluation.** Take time to go over the problems in class. Subsequent papers will be much more carefully written, and you will be able to write briefer comments because of the shared class understanding of what you expect.

- **Limit tutorial time.** Students usually can work on only so much at one time. After 20–30 minutes, let the student go home to work on what you have been teaching in that conference. You can schedule another appointment to address other issues.

- **Get started on the papers as soon as possible.** Sometimes the hardest part of reading papers is starting the task. Try to grade at least one or two on the day the papers come in, to get over the inertia. Always return the papers within a week, unless they are very long. If you wait too long to return papers, the students will not be as likely to learn from your comments. It's better to make fewer comments and return the papers soon, than to cover the pages with comments and return them late.

- **Discover your optimal working pattern.** Some teachers like to grade a few papers a day; others like to grade a whole class set in one sitting. Some like to grade early in the day; others prefer to do it late at night. Find out what works best for you. (Note: Even if you think you "work well under pressure," don't procrastinate grading until two hours before you must return the papers.)

- **Sit in a comfortable location.** Work wherever you feel comfortable—at your desk, at a library table, on the couch, or on a lawn chair in the sun. Change locations sometimes to give yourself a break. Moving from the desk to a comfortable chair sometimes can give you the energy to go on for another hour or two.

- **Reward yourself.** After every so many papers, go for a walk, eat a cookie, or talk to a friend. One of my colleagues hides M & Ms in his stack of papers so that every so often he comes across one and can eat it.

- **Remind yourself that this is what you're paid for.**

- **Get to know your students.** Think of reading and responding to the papers as a conversation. The students have spoken with you through their papers, and now you can answer their ideas through your comments. Once you think of it that way, it can become a labor of love, as one of my colleagues put it.

Conclusion

Teaching writing, especially responding to and evaluating writing, is time consuming. But teaching well can save you time, and good time-management skills can help you to grade more efficiently. Most of all, if you care about what your students are saying in their writing, you can actually enjoy reading and responding to their work.

In fact, caring about your students is the key to all aspects of being a good TA. Care enough to listen to what students are trying to communicate and to help them find the best way to present those ideas in a particular piece of writing. Have faith that each student has something unique to contribute to the class conversation on a topic. Look forward to learning from each student.

Robert Frost said, "I'm not a teacher, but an awakener." A TA in a writing-intensive class can be the one who awakens in students the desire and ability to share their understanding with others. Enjoy being an awakener.

Chapter Checklist

☐ Use the principles in the book to teach more efficiently. Preparing students to write well will save time in the long run.

☐ Remember the purpose of the responding/grading for each piece you work on. This will help you to use your time more effectively.

☐ Discipline yourself not to spend too much time on each paper. Remember that you need to comment on only the most important areas for revision.

☐ Care about your students. Enjoy the opportunity to carry on a conversation with each one.

Applications to Your Own Situation

1. Practice some of the time-saving techniques listed in this chapter and throughout this book. Determine which ones work best for you. Think of new techniques that will help you use your time as efficiently and effectively as you can.

2. Consider what kind of response and evaluation each writing assignment requires. Which ones require formative responses? Summative comments?

3. For each assignment that you will grade, decide beforehand how many minutes you will spend on each paper and try to keep within those parameters.

Working with Your Professor

1. Work with your professor to institute some of these time-saving strate-
    gies, especially including intermediate assignments leading up to a
    major paper and using class time to teach writing skills to the group.
2. Discuss with your professor if you feel the expectations are too great for
    the time you are working. Your professor may not have a realistic idea
    of the time required to do what he or she has asked you to do.

Notes

CHAPTER 1

1. Peter Elbow, "Ranking, Evaluating, and Liking: Sorting Out Three Forms of Judgment," *College English* 55 (1993): 200.

CHAPTER 2

1. Janet Emig, "Writing as a Mode of Learning," *College Composition and Communication* 28 (1977): 122–28.

2. Toby Fulwiler, qtd. in Toni-Lee Capossela, *The Harcourt Brace Guide to Peer Tutoring* (New York: Harcourt Brace, 1998) 22.

3. Paula Gillespie, "E-Journals: Writing to Learn in the Literature Classroom," *Electronic Communication across the Curriculum*, eds. Donna Reiss, Dickie Selfe, and Art Young (Urbana: NCTE, 1998) 221–30.

4. Robert Wolffe, "Math Learning through Electronic Journaling," *Electronic Communication across the Curriculum*, eds. Donna Reiss, Dickie Selfe, and Art Young (Urbana: NCTE, 1998) 273–81.

5. Deborah M. Langsam and Kathleen Blake Yancey, "E-mailing Biology: Facing the Biochallenge," *Electronic Communication across the Curriculum*, eds. Donna Reiss, Dickie Selfe, and Art Young (Urbana: NCTE, 1998) 231–41.

6. Barbara Walvoord, *Helping Students Write Well: A Guide for Teachers in All Disciplines*, 2nd ed. (New York: MLA, 1986) 5.

CHAPTER 3

1. Linda Flowers and John R. Hayes, "The Cognition of Discovery: Defining a Rhetorical Problem," *The Harcourt Brace Guide to Peer Tutoring*, ed. Toni-Lee Capossela (New York: Harcourt Brace, 1998) 155–56.

2. Leigh Ryan, *The Bedford Guide for Writing Tutors*, 3rd ed. (Boston: Bedford/St. Martin's, 2002) 60–62.

CHAPTER 4

1. David Porush, *A Short Guide to Writing about Science* (New York: Longman, 1995) 6.

2. William Strunk, Jr. and E. B. White, *The Elements of Style*, 4th ed. (Boston: Allyn & Bacon, 2000) 15.

3. Gayle E. Tompkins, *Teaching Writing: Balancing Process and Product* (New York: Macmillan, 1994) 184–87.

4. Strunk and White, iv.

5. Dee Unglaub Silverthorn, *Human Physiology: An Integrated Approach*, 2nd ed. (Upper Saddle River: Prentice Hall, 2001) 327.

6. Jared Diamond, *Guns, Germs, and Steel: The Fates of Human Societies* (New York: Norton, 1999) 90.

7. Charles Standard and Dale Davis, *Running Today's Factory: A Proven Strategy for Lean Manufacturing* (Dearborn: Society of Manufacturing Engineers, 1999) 117.

8. John R. Trimble, *Writing with Style: Conversations on the Art of Writing*, 2nd ed. (Upper Saddle River: Prentice Hall, 2000) 8.

CHAPTER 5

1. *A State of Confusion: Students Talk about Writing*, prod. and dir. Steven W. Olpin, videocassette, Brigham Young University, Coll. of General Ed. and Honors, 1993.

2. Nancy Sommers, "Revision Strategies of Student Writers and Experienced Adult Writers," *Teaching Composition: Background Readings*, eds. T. R. Johnson and Shirley Morahan (Boston: Bedford/St. Martin's, 2002) 223–26.

3. Karen Spear, *Sharing Writing: Peer Response Groups in English Classes* (Portsmouth: Boynton/Cook, 1987) 132.

4. Pamela Flash and Lee-Ann Kastman Breuch, "Face-to-Face and Screen-to-Screen," Writing Across the Curriculum Conf., Rice University, Houston, 9 Mar. 2002.

5. John Updike, qtd. in John R. Trimble, *Writing with Style: Conversations on the Art of Writing*, 2nd ed. (Upper Saddle River: Prentice Hall, 2000) 183.

6. Ellen Goodman, qtd. in Trimble, *Writing with Style*, 171.

CHAPTER 6

1. George Orwell, qtd. in John R. Trimble, *Writing with Style: Conversations on the Art of Writing*, 2nd ed. (Upper Saddle River: Prentice Hall, 2000) 179.

2. David Porush, *A Short Guide to Writing about Science* (New York: Longman, 1995) 12.

3. Sharon Friedman and Stephen Steinberg, *Writing and Thinking in the Social Sciences* (Englewood Cliffs: Prentice Hall, 1989) 32–34.

CHAPTER 10

1. Edward B. Jenkinson and Donald A. Seybold, prologue, *Writing as a Process of Discovery: Some Structured Theme Assignments for Grades Five through Twelve* (Bloomington: Indiana UP, 1970) pp. 3–6, qtd. In Erika Lindemann, *A Rhetoric for Writing Teachers*, 3rd Ed. (New York: Oxford University Press, 1995) 225.

2. Vicki Spandel and Richard J. Stiggins, qtd. in John Bean, *Engaging Ideas: The Professor's Guide to Integrating Writing, Critical Thinking, and Active Learning in the Classroom* (San Francisco: Jossey-Bass, 2001) 240–41.

3. Nancy Sommers, "Responding to Student Writing," *Teaching Composition: Background Readings*, eds. T. R. Johnson and Shirley Morahan (Boston: Bedford/St. Martin's, 2002) 353.

4. Ibid., 356.

5. Beth Hoger, "Invisible Decisions as Instructors Write Commentary," Conf. on Coll. Composition and Communication Convention, Atlanta, 1999.

6. Chris M. Anson, "Reflective Reading: Developing Thoughtful Ways to Respond to Students' Writing," *Evaluating Writing: The Role of Teachers' Knowledge about Text, Learning, and Culture*, eds. Charles R. Cooper and Lee Odell (Urbana: NCTE, 1999) 302.

7. Peter Elbow, *Writing without Teachers* (New York: Oxford University Press, 1973) 85.

8. Adapted from Toni-Lee Capossela, *The Harcourt Brace Guide to Peer Tutoring* (New York: Harcourt Brace, 1998) 12.

9. Robert Connors and Cheryl Glenn, *The New St. Martin's Guide to Teaching Writing* (Boston: Bedford/St. Martin's, 1999) 103.

10. Ibid., 105.

CHAPTER 11

1. David Porush, *A Short Guide to Writing about Science* (New York: Longman, 1995) 48–62.

2. Kathleen Medina, "Evaluating Student Writing about History," *Evaluating Writing: The Role of Teachers' Knowledge about Text, Learning, and Culture*, eds. Charles R. Cooper and Lee Odell (Urbana: NCTE, 1999) 170–94.

3. Edward M. White, *Teaching and Assessing Writing: Recent Advances in Understanding, Evaluating, and Improving Student Performance* (San Francisco: Jossey-Bass, 1994) 9.

4. Robert Connors and Cheryl Glenn, *The New St. Martin's Guide to Teaching Writing* (Boston: Bedford/St. Martin's, 1999) 107.

CHAPTER 12

1. Christian M. Reiner, Timothy W. Bothell, and Richard R. Sudweeks, *Preparing Effective Essay Questions: A Self-Directed Workbook for Educators* (Stillwater: New Forums Press, 2003) 12.

2. Ibid., 20.

3. Ibid.

4. Edward M. White, *Teaching and Assessing Writing: Recent Advances in Understanding, Evaluating, and Improving Student Performance* (San Francisco: Jossey-Bass, 1994) 29.

5. Edward M. White, *Assigning, Responding, and Evaluating: A Writing Teacher's Guide*, 3rd ed. (Boston: Bedford/St. Martin's, 1999) 29.

6. John Bean, *Engaging Ideas: The Professor's Guide to Integrating Writing, Critical Thinking, and Active Learning in the Classroom* (San Francisco: Jossey-Bass, 2001) 192.

7. Ibid.

8. White, *Teaching*, 59.

9. Bean, 191.

10. Reiner, Bothell, and Sudweeks, 33.

11. Bean, 193.

12. Ibid., 194–95.

13. Tom Romano, *Clearing the Way: Working with Teenage Writers* (Portsmouth: Heinemann, 1987) 54.

CHAPTER 13

1. Rebecca Moore Howard, "Forget about Policing Plagiarism. Just *Teach*," *The Chronicle of Higher Education* 16 Nov. 2001: B24.

2. Ibid.

3. Robert A. Harris, *The Plagiarism Handbook: Strategies for Preventing, Detecting, and Dealing with Plagiarism* (Los Angeles: Pyrczak, 2001) 61–81.

4. Alan Brinkley, Betty Dessants, Michael Flamm, Cynthia Fleming, Charles Forcy, and Eric Rothschild, *The Chicago Handbook for Teachers: A Practical Guide to the College Classroom* (Chicago: University of Chicago Press, 1999) 124–25.

CHAPTER 14

1. Elizabeth A. Martinez and Daniel P. Hallahan, "Education of Individuals with Learning Disabilities," *Encyclopedia of Education*, ed. James W. Guthrie, 2nd ed. (New York: MacMillan, 2002).

2. *Understanding Students with Learning or Attention Disabilities* (Provo: Brigham Young University Accessibility Center, 2003).

3. Ana Preto-Bay, "Teaching International Students," *Writing Matters: The BYU GE Newsletter on Writing across the Curriculum* 3.4 (2002): 2.

4. Diane Strong-Krause, "Strategies to Benefit English as a Second Language Students," *Writing Matters: The BYU GE Newsletter on Writing across the Curriculum* 3.4 (2002): 1.

5. Robert B. Kaplan, foreword, *Contrastive Rhetoric Revisited and Redefined*, ed. Clayann Gilliam Panetta (Mahwah: Lawrence Erlbaum Associates, 2001) xii.

6. Robert B. Kaplan, "Cultural Thought Patterns in Inter-Cultural Education," *Language Learning* 16 (1966): 15.

7. Lynn M. Goldstein and Susan M. Conrad, "Student Input and Negotiation of Meaning in ESL Writing Conferences," *TESOL Quarterly* 24 (1990): 457.

8. Rik Andes, "When English Becomes an Obstacle: Strategies for Working with ESL Students," unpublished handout, Brigham Young University, 2002.

9. Marilyn J. Valentino, "Responding When a Life Depends on It: What to Write in the Margins When Students Self-Disclose," *TETYC* 23.4 (1996): 274–283.

10. Ibid., 280.

11. Ibid.

12. Elizabeth Birmingham, "Gender Differences in Grading Style and TA Response to Student Papers," *In Our Own Voice: Graduate Students Teach Writing*, eds. Tina Lavonne Good and Leanne B. Warshauer (Boston: Allyn & Bacon, 2000) 208.

13. Ibid., 209.

14. Alan Brinkley, Betty Dessants, Michael Flamm, Cynthia Fleming, Charles Forcy, and Eric Rothschild, *The Chicago Handbook for Teachers: A Practical Guide to the College Classroom* (Chicago: University of Chicago Press, 1999) 126–27.

Bibliography

PROFESSIONAL RESOURCES FROM BEDFORD/ST. MARTIN'S

Bizzel, Patricia, Bruce Herzberg, and Nedra Reynolds. *The Bedford Bibliography for Teachers of Writing*. 6th ed. Boston: Bedford/St. Martin's, 2003.

Bullock, Richard. *The St. Martin's Manual for Writing in the Disciplines: A Guide for Faculty*. New York: St. Martin's, 1994.

Glenn, Cheryl, Melissa A. Goldthwaite, and Robert Connors. *The St. Martin's Guide to Teaching Writing*. Boston: Bedford/St. Martin's, 2003.

Johnson, T. R., and Shirley Morahan, eds. *Teaching Composition: Background Readings*. Boston: Bedford/St. Martin's, 2002.

Murphy, Christina, and Steve Sherwood. *The St. Martin's Sourcebook for Writing Tutors*. 2nd ed. Boston: Bedford/St. Martin's, 2003.

Ryan, Leigh. *The Bedford Guide for Writing Tutors*. 3rd ed. Boston: Bedford/St. Martin's, 2002.

White, Edward M. *Assigning, Responding, and Evaluating: A Writing Teacher's Guide*. 3rd ed. Boston: Bedford/St. Martin's, 1999.

WRITING HANDBOOKS

Beason, Larry, and Mark Lester. *A Commonsense Guide to Grammar and Usage*. 3rd ed. Boston: Bedford/St. Martin's, 2003.

Hacker, Diana. *The Bedford Handbook*. 6th ed. Boston: Bedford/St. Martin's, 2002.

———. *A Pocket Style Manual*. 3rd ed. Boston: Bedford/St. Martin's, 2000.

———. *Rules for Writers*. 4th ed. Boston: Bedford/St. Martin's, 2000.

———. *A Writer's Reference*. 5th ed. Boston: Bedford/St. Martin's, 2003.

Lunsford, Andrea A. *EasyWriter*. 2nd ed. Boston: Bedford/St. Martin's, 2002.

———. *The Everyday Writer*. 2nd ed. Boston: Bedford/St. Martin's, 2001.

———. *The St. Martin's Handbook*. 5th ed. Boston: Bedford/St. Martin's, 2003.

DISCIPLINE-SPECIFIC WRITING GUIDES

Barnet, Sylvan. *A Short Guide to Writing about Art*. 7th ed. New York: Longman, 2002.

Becker, Howard S. *Writing for Social Scientists*. Chicago: U of Chicago P, 1986.

Bellman, Jonathan. *A Short Guide to Writing about Music*. New York: Longman, 2000.

Benjamin, Jules R. *A Student's Guide to History*. 9th ed. Boston: Bedford/St. Martin's, 2003.

Corrigan, Timothy. *A Short Guide to Writing about Film*. 4th ed. New York: Longman, 2004.

Dunn, Dana. *A Short Guide to Writing about Psychology*. New York: Longman, 2004.

McMillan, Victoria E. *Writing Papers in the Biological Sciences*. 3rd ed. Boston, Bedford/St. Martin's, 2001.

Porush, David. *A Short Guide to Writing about Science*. New York: Longman, 1995.

Winsor, Dorothy. *Writing Like an Engineer: A Rhetorical Education*. Mahwah: Lawrence Erlbaum Associates, 1996.

DISCIPLINE-SPECIFIC STYLE AND DOCUMENTATION GUIDES

American Chemical Society. *The ACS Style Guide: A Manual for Authors and Editors*. Ed. Janet S. Dodd. 2nd ed. New York: Oxford UP, 1997.

American Institute of Physics. *AIP Style Manual*. 4th ed. New York: Amer. Inst. of Physics, 1990.

American Mathematical Society. *AMS Author Handbook*. Providence: Amer. Mathematical Soc., 1997.

The Chicago Manual of Style. 15th ed. Chicago: U of Chicago P, 2003.

Council of Biology Editors. *Scientific Style and Format: The CBE Manual for Authors, Editors, and Publishers*. Ed. Edward J. Huth. 6th ed. New York: Cambridge UP, 1994.

Gibaldi, Joseph. *MLA Handbook for Writers of Research Papers*. 6th ed. New York: MLA, 2003.

Publication Manual of the American Psychological Association. 5th ed. Washington: APA, 2001.

United States Geological Survey. *Suggestions to Authors of the Reports of the United States Geological Survey*. 7th ed. Washington: GPO, 1991.

GENERAL STYLE AND EDITING GUIDES

Lanham, Richard. *Revising Prose*. 4th ed. Boston: Allyn & Bacon, 2000.

Strunk, William, Jr., and E. B. White. *The Elements of Style*. 4th ed. Boston: Allyn & Bacon, 2000.

Trimble, John. *Writing with Style: Conversation on the Art of Writing*. 2nd ed. Upper Saddle River: Prentice Hall, 2000.

Williams, Joseph. *Style: Ten Lessons in Clarity and Grace*. 6th ed. New York: Longman, 2000.

Zinsser, William. *On Writing Well*. 7th ed. New York: Harper, 2001.

TEACHING RESOURCES AND REFERENCES

Bean, John. *Engaging Ideas: The Professor's Guide to Integrating Writing, Critical Thinking, and Active Learning in the Classroom.* San Francisco: Jossey-Bass, 2001.

Brinkley, Alan, Betty Dessants, Michael Flamm, Cynthia Fleming, Charles Forcy, and Eric Rothschild. *The Chicago Handbook for Teachers: A Practical Guide to the College Classroom.* Chicago: U of Chicago P, 1999.

Capossela, Toni-Lee. *The Harcourt Brace Guide to Peer Tutoring.* New York: Harcourt, 1998.

Cooper, Charles R., and Lee Odell, eds. *Evaluating Writing: The Role of Teachers' Knowledge about Text, Learning, and Culture.* Urbana: NCTE, 1999.

Dethier, Brock. *The Composition Instructor's Survival Guide.* Portsmouth: Boynton/Cook, 1999.

Elbow, Peter. *Writing without Teachers.* 2nd ed. New York: Oxford UP, 1998.

Fulwiler, Toby. *The Journal Book.* Portsmouth: Boynton/Cook, 1987.

Gardner, Susan, and Toby Fulwiler, eds. *The Journal Book for Teachers in Technical and Professional Programs.* Portsmouth: Heinemann, 1999.

Gilliam Panetta, Clayann, ed. *Contrastive Rhetoric Revisited and Redefined.* Mahwah: Lawrence Erlbaum Associates, 2001.

Good, Tina Lavonne, and Leanne B. Warshauer, eds. *In Our Own Voice: Graduate Students Teach Writing.* Boston: Allyn & Bacon, 2000.

Harris, Robert A. *The Plagiarism Handbook: Strategies for Preventing, Detecting, and Dealing with Plagiarism.* Los Angeles: Pyrczak, 2001.

Lanham, Richard. *Revising Prose.* 2nd ed. New York: Macmillan, 1987.

Lindemann, Erika. *A Rhetoric for Writing Teachers.* 3rd ed. New York: Oxford UP, 1995.

Reiss, Donna, Dickie Selfe, and Art Young, eds. *Electronic Communication Across the Curriculum.* Urbana: NCTE, 1998.

Romano, Tom. *Clearing the Way: Working with Teenage Writers.* Portsmouth: Heinemann, 1987.

Spear, Karen. *Sharing Writing: Peer Response Groups in English Classes.* Portsmouth: Boynton/Cook, 1988.

Tompkins, Gayle E. *Teaching Writing: Balancing Process and Product.* New York: Macmillan, 1994.

Walvoord, Barbara. *Helping Students Write Well: A Guide for Teachers in All Disciplines.* 2nd ed. New York: MLA, 1986.

White, Edward M. *Teaching and Assessing Writing: Recent Advances in Understanding, Evaluating, and Improving Student Performance.* San Francisco: Jossey-Bass, 1994.

Index